I Quit Being A Christian To Follow Jesus

By
Alan Scott

Table Of Contents

Author's Note

This is a study based on and birthed out of the New Testament book of Luke. Each chapter begins with a brief section of Luke recalled. I highly recommend you don't skip over these verses like I'm usually inclined to do when I pick up a book with sections of scripture reprinted.

In fact, I think if you skip and skim over the scripture, you'll be less likely to get the point.

Here's my point: read the scripture. It's the best part of this book anyway.

Prologue

It was at an Owl City concert where I realized there had to be more. My enlightening concert experience also became a living metaphor for my Christianity. Somewhere between the music and my religion, I quit being a Christian to follow Jesus. Let me explain...

My three teenage daughter's music has always been a strange and curious world for me to peek into. From a safe distance I am allowed to remain both cool and Dad, while indulging myself in their music. I don't believe their music will ever be as classic as mine. Will anyone ever equal such soulful powerhouses as the Eagles, Boston, or Styx? Please. Of course, the term "classic" is painfully relative with my girls. They seem to relegate my world of classic to their definition of just plain old. That really hurts.

Occasionally, I attempt to dive into their world of new and hip music. Sometimes my girls, Brooklynn, Lauren and Morgan, even encourage my efforts. I don't take this lightly. Entering the arena of my kids' music is a journey onto holy ground. Somewhere along the way, my girls became guarded music snobs (One of them even wears a t-shirt which says: "I listen to bands that don't even exist yet.").

Not too long ago, I was introduced to a Minnesota-based band called Owl City. Approximately six months before the obnoxious masses discovered Adam Young and his retro-synth sound, all the Scotts were bopping in the minivan to his Owl City song, "Fireflies." My girls still enjoy reminding me of their musical unearthing genius every time "Fireflies" comes blaring through the radio.

When Adam Young and Owl City came to town, my girls graciously invited me to go to the concert with them. I was on to them. Their invitation was not as warm and fuzzy as it initially sounded. I was merely the free transportation needed. Because I actually began grooving to Owl City, I was quick to jump on this fun opportunity to hear a new band, and spend some time with kids I thoroughly enjoy.

The concert was held in a smaller, dark, cavernous, and extremely young venue in downtown Atlanta. A crowd of about 500 people gathered to thump along with Owl City. I swear my pant leg was flapping by the sub woofers as I mixed in with the crowd. Of course, my daughters were beginning to wonder where all of these invasive people were coming from. Nobody else was supposed to know about this hidden pop sensation.

The evening grew a bit long and late for dad. However, I didn't want to leave without hearing the eventual Billboard chart-topping "Fireflies." With my car keys in hand, I finally heard the familiar synthesizer intro and Adam Young's vocals energizing the thumpin' urban audience. "You would not believe your eyes, if ten million fireflies…"

Probably 20 seconds into the song, the band just stopped. Owl City arrogantly walked off the stage. Everyone thought it just a prankish taunt to manufacture a cheap encore. Nope. That was it. The lights went up and the concert was officially over. A stunned audience was trying to figure out what just happened. Most were convinced there was going to be more, while others finished the song with an accapella, spontaneous, off-pitch rendition. Although I was beyond ready to go home, I felt cheated. There really should have been more. A hungry audience wanted more. Even a dad out of his aging element wanted more.

Lately I've felt like being a modern day Christian has left me wanting more. A growing constituency of "others" want more. My suburban, American world has a finely developed and lucrative subculture of what a Christian should look like, wear, listen to, read, and decorate his or her car with. Sometimes, because our corporate gatherings have become so predictably programmed, I've questioned if God has left us to drown in our own designs. Meanwhile, He's moved on to oversee some really awesome things in places like China where Jesus is actually the point.

I titled this book with a hopeful edge because I wanted to connect with someone like you who has similar internal groans. You want more. I actually like the term *Christian*; it's what this barely-Biblical word has become that pains me. Church people in the first century were called Christians first in a city named Antioch (Acts 11:26). Their identity in Jesus was with Godly pride, personal conviction, and the very real threat of death. Being a Christian was a passionate pursuit to imitate Jesus. However, as Os Guinness writes, "Christian is certainly a term used in the New Testament, but by outsiders and with the suggestion of an insult. To others, Christians were

Christianoi --- 'Messiah's men.' But among themselves, the preferred term for disciples was followers of Jesus or followers of the Way. There was no 'Christianity' abroad on the earth, only a radical, new 'Way' and a motley band of 'brothers' and 'sisters' who were 'followers of the Way.'"[1]

These days, people outside the Church don't see Christians as such. We're being labeled as bubble-dwelling, homophobic, hard-to-get-along-with, conservative, non-relevant jerks. It seems our beloved title of *Christian* has been hi-jacked not by masked terrorists, but rather by half-hearted believers who like Jesus as Savior but not specifically as Lord and Master.

The strategies needed to battle this sad maligning have been slow in coming. In the mean time, I have quit being a *Christian*, and hope to simply follow Jesus as Lord, Master, and Savior. Reclaiming a life befitting the label won't be an easy task, but practical help is found within the amazing dynamics of the Bible. I happen to like what Dr. Luke writes in the New Testament. He seems to bring us back to powerful basics that help to define both *Christian* and *Jesus Follower*.

I know there's more. Don't you really know this too? That fish on the back of your car really DOES mean something. Its purpose should be more than merely enticing someone to honk and wish you a nice day if, indeed, you didn't just cut them off. The concert isn't over. The best music --- the music and song we long to hear --- has not disappeared or been rerouted to China. We've just stepped strangely and temporarily off the stage. I sense God wants to bring us back for a fist-pumping encore. Let's scream, cheer, write, pray, search, and hunger until the real music plays again. There is soon to be more music reverberating a challenging melody. Maybe Christians and Jesus followers everywhere will raise their Bic lighters into the air and begin wearing, again, the impeccable name of Jesus. Let's explore some specific strategies to help get us there.

Prologue End Notes

1. Os Guinness, <u>The Call: Finding And Fulfilling The Central Purpose Of Your Life</u> (Nashville, TN, Thomas Nelson 1998) pg. 109-110.

Chapter One -

PB & Jesus

Strategy #1: Revive or gain your certainty of faith.

Luke 1:1-4

"Many have undertaken to draw up an account of the things that have been fulfilled among us, just as they were handed down to us by those who from the first were eyewitnesses and servants of the word. Therefore, since I myself have carefully investigated everything from the beginning, it seemed good also to me to write an orderly account for you, most excellent Theophilus, so that you may know the certainty of the things you have been taught."

How would you persuade me to make a peanut butter and jelly masterpiece if I were from another planet?

For the sake of argument, let's say you are blind folded. I have all the essential PB & J elements in a brown paper bag. Now go ahead; convince, persuade, and instruct a dumb-but-anxious alien. I have never had a peanut butter and jelly sandwich, but I've heard they are really, really good.

Would you start by asking me to open the jar of peanut butter? I don't know what a jar is, and I've never seen peanut butter. What if I decided the knife must be what you call the peanut butter? Confused yet? What if you told me to open the bread, and I asked, "What is bread?" This is going to get frustrating very quickly, isn't it? As you tell me to open up the soft, squishy stuff you call bread, I rip open the bag and grab most of the entire loaf. Twisty ties have not yet come to my planet. You might tell me to put the brown, creamy stuff on the bread, and I would roll the jar back and forth on top of the bread. How would you get me to apply the jelly and use a spoon, if I didn't know what a spoon or jelly was? Remember, you're doing this blindfolded to a curious but non-earth dweller. Can you imagine the exhausting mess we would have once your blind-fold is removed and your eyes could see what YOU helped create?

How would you persuade someone off the street who is a spiritual alien to consider the Bible and Christianity? If you were theologically blind folded, how would you explain faith, the Bible, and Jesus? Could you do it, or would that curious and hungry alien have more of a confusing mess than before he bravely inquired?

Gaining a viable, convincing, and street-wise faith in Jesus is what the New Testament book of Luke is all about. If you're a tired Christian but also a wanna-be Jesus follower, Dr. Luke has some practical gems to boost your faith. On the other hand, if you're the exploring spiritual alien, there are also some answers within this ancient doctor's inspired pen. If by chance (or perhaps divine providence) you're reading this book as a skeptic, you're going to have some ammunition to enable a very healthy and potentially life-changing conversation.

The writer of Luke (& Acts) is a friendly, likeable doctor (Colossians 4:14). Maybe you didn't catch the intended irony. He was a physician people actually liked. When was the last time you had your doctor over for some friendly fried catfish, grits, and sweet, southern tea?

First and foremost, Luke is a skilled doctor; second, he's a friend. The combination of studious wit and depth of relationship is a rarity for in any century.

In the first century there was a notable school in the city of Alexandria, Egypt. This was a medical college. This place of ancient, higher education boasted a great faculty with wisdom from Greek, Roman, Babylonian, and Indian schools of thought. Some people believe Dr. Luke grew to be a recognized, pipe-smoking intellectual exactly because his wall diploma touted this prestigious school. Graduates of this particular school in Alexandria had a wealth of information concerning medicine and science. So we know Dr. Luke was smart. (In a Cliff Clavin "Cheers" kind of way, you should know just how smart this Luke guy really was. He uses 800 smart words nobody else uses in the entire New Testament. Bust out that little-known fact on your next fun-filled Bible trivia night!) Along with being a brainiac, he was also a good friend, which means he was not so smart that he didn't have any common sense. He could relate to people like you and me.

Additionally, the Bible gives us hints that our potentially captivating doctor was a hard worker with old-fashioned work ethics (Luke 1:1-3). Translation: Dr. Luke didn't play much golf. Imagine that. But wait... there's more. He was smart, friendly, a hard-worker, and packed along more than his share of fortitude. Do you remember fortitude before it was hung only as a motivational poster in corporate offices? Dr. Luke could stick with something. Marriage. Parenting. Church. God. He didn't quit like I am sadly bent to do. I am attracted to the kind of solid character Luke displayed.

Subsequently our good doctor, Luke, was a really good candidate for God to choose in writing most of His New Testament. By sheer volume, Luke wrote most of the New Testament with two efforts we call Luke and Acts. If you're the Creator of the universe saying, "I'm looking for qualified people to write My Book," Luke is a good find. If you're God, you've just selected a very worthy writer when you pinpoint Luke.

Are you intrigued enough to dig in and see what this guy has to say? You game? I'm hoping that inquisitive alien standing on your doorstep is giving you a bit of motivation.

Here's one extremely personal note about why I particularly like this writer of the third gospel. He's not Jewish. I have absolutely no prejudice against Jewish folks. It's just that Luke is special because he's non-Jewish. Out of all the hand-selected writers of the New Testament, there's only one person who's not a Jewish person. It's Dr. Luke. You can view Luke as somewhat of an outcast. This is appealing to me. There have been far too many times in my life when I've felt like an outcast to NOT relate to a guy like

Luke. I'm confident you've experienced those kinds of exiled times too.

In the weird-but-exhilarating days just out of high school, I was in a dry spell of dating. Four or five other friends were living in that same dating desert. We banded together and made a desperate attempt to attract. We started a club called the "Lone Wolf Club." It was basically a bunch of sorry, lonely guys who said, "You know, we're tired of being excluded, so let's start a dumb, pitiful club." We hung out together on Friday nights and talked about the girls we wanted to date and the guys we hated who were dating those same ignorant, obviously deluded girls. Why did we start this really dumb, pitiful club? Because we just wanted to be included.

Sometimes religion and church can exclude and separate like an Amish family at a car dealership. Have you felt that churchy loneliness before? Dr. Luke is an inclusive writer. In the "I Helped Write The Bible" fraternity, Dr. Luke is an outsider. He knows exactly how many of us feel. Luke has an uncanny way of connecting the unconnected like women and common laborers and Greeks and Samaritans. These were people who were, in the first century, viewed as throw away bums. Our highlighted physician looks at such deemed losers and says, "Come on in. The water is fine." While some marginalized type people may venture into the darkness of a bar in hopes of encountering relationship, Dr. Luke says to all who are harshly excluded, "Come into my book. Come into my letter, and you will encounter Jesus."

Just what is Dr. Luke's motivation with all of this? What's he actually trying to accomplish? Simply put, he's trying to create a spiritual PB & J work of art with an alien by the name of Theophilus. How many guys with that name can you find in the phone book? He must be from another planet! A pastor on staff at our church decided to name his son Owen Theophilus in honor of our new series in Luke. Poor kid! You know that's gonna bite him on some fateful day in junior high.

In the first century, Theophilus meant "Friend of God." Our Biblical alien, Theophilus, was a real, elected, educated, and "excellent" Roman officer surrounded by Jewish people in a religious and Jewish world. Luke was focusing on a Roman-world big dawg who was made to feel small and insignificant by the popular church world. Luke must have been a good friend to this spiritually hungry Roman officer. Doc Luke wanted to build his faith in Jesus.

Luke was privy to stories and oral traditions about Jesus that had been handed down and passed around. Luke had an insider's take on things like Jesus's teaching, miracles, death, burial, and resurrection. He was able to apply his training, formal education, relational bend, work ethic, and fortitude in digging into such weighty matters. Luke investigated and wrote to shore up the faith of people outside of a boxy, predictable religious culture. By the way, that same lifeless religion required little to no faith then as well as today. This culture of stale religion began to taint and undermine the name *Christian*, so Luke put pen to paper. Now you understand better the motivation behind this book.

Dr. Luke writes to redefine or correct what being a *Christian* had become. Luke and the strangely-named Theophilus want to turn shaky things of faith into a certainty. They want to help spiritual aliens make peanut butter and Jesus sandwiches. For an outsider like Theophilus, this book would have been such a vital and welcome read. Our investigation into this awesome gospel is similar: *"...so that you may know the certainty of the things you have been taught."*

Like me, you've probably been stuck in a cesspool of spiritual uncertainty. Too often my quest for answers ends up with the inevitable, dreaded Bible glaze. The onslaught of the Bible glaze hits you when you're trying to search and read the Bible. After tackling an entire chapter of an eenie-meenie-minee-mo selected passage, you come crawling to the end. At that point you embarrassingly whisper, "I have no idea what I just read." You just read every word, buuuuut you have no heavenly clue as to what's being said. The Bible glaze builds no confidence when our search is already uncertain. Have no fear, grasshopper. Through Luke's unique wiring and circumstance, our Bible glaze is greatly minimized because this doc seems to enjoy busting through religious protocol and insider information. You and your new companion, Theophilus, are going to actually have a bit of fun reading the Bible as you read Luke, I promise.

I've wondered if Theophilus found Jesus in a rough, hard, unconventional way. What about you?

Maybe after accepting Jesus as Lord, Theophilus been knocked back a bit by religion, politics, and loneliness. Perhaps Theo (feels like I actually know this guy) needs practical evidence for the credibility of what he believes. Maybe he's had a spiritual alien asking about the elusive peanut butter and Jesus sandwich. There's a real need for a defense and explanation of his faith. Wouldn't a spiritual certainty be a welcome glass of milk for the whole PB & J exercise?

A while back, I went to a bit stuffy gathering called *The Case for Faith Seminar* in Atlanta. A really smart man by the name of Dr. George Jacobian spoke. His dubious topic was: *Is the Bible Trustworthy?* It had my name written all over it. Literally. Somehow my name was put on a colorful mailer dropped onto my desk. I was being beckoned. I also struggled with throwing away a mailer touting God and the Bible. How do you ignore and flip something like this into the trashcan? Welcome to my inner most office space likely needing attention from a good counselor.

What IS the certainty of the authority and infallibility of Scripture? Sound fun? I went to my wife and I said, "Hey, Sherry baby-honey! Let's go! We can make a date of it. We'll go out to eat at a fancy fast-food place, and then we'll take in this great seminar. It will be really good. It will be like a date." That was my hard sell. It was the "like a date" idea, which began my romantic downfall. Sherry placated a bit, but eventually responded with an unconvinced, "What's the topic?" I told her. Exactly because she loves and understands me, Sherry finished me off with a firm, "Maybe next time." "But Sherry," I begged, "this is how pastors woo their wives. Come on, it's the authority and the infallibility of Scripture, baby!"

I went alone. Feeling somewhat like the outcast Theophilus, I soaked in Jacobian's eight reasons why the Bible can be trusted. Here's the quick, fast version so you don't get that glaze thing again:

1. *The Bible is honest.* You should think about this one for just a minute. The Bible is full of criminals and murderers and rapists and you-name-it lowlifes. None of these colorful characters are hidden in some spiritual closet as shameful dirty laundry. If you were trying to prove the sureness of this Book, why would you put that stuff in there? Stop for a mere second. You should pause to chew on this little taste of the wonderful credibility and brutal honesty of Scriptures. The integrity of the Bible is like the orchestral music underscoring of an epic movie. The story just wouldn't be the same without it.

2. *Its unique in preservation.* Over the years and in my lifetime there have been lots of people who have tried to diminish or destroy the Bible. It just does not happen. In fact, did you know the Bible is still at the top of the top of all lists of best-sellers? This is formidable information. However, you won't see the Bible on the actual best-sellers list because people gave up listing it over and over again, year after year. It's number one always. Over 40 million Bibles are sold each year in America alone. It's extremely unique in its preservation. God's story has endured, even though religion tends to bury it.

3. *Its claims are both divine and human.* God created the Bible through humans. That's a very distinctive dynamic. Deal with it. God's has written a great play and we are the actors and actresses. In fact, some have even been on the writing team. Make no mistake, it's God's story and we're invited to swim in its massive implications. This means the story is both large and intimate. How cool is that?

4. *The miracles found within the Book have evidence to back them up.* Carl Sagan once said, "Extraordinary claims require extraordinary evidence."[1] Luke's book offers really cool evidence as we will see. A God who comes to Earth to redeem from the curse of sin AND offer full restoration is the spectacular saga Luke set out to prove. His careful investigation of historical eyewitnesses must be viewed as just south of "da bomb." Francis Schaeffer wrote, "Every honest question must be given an honest answer. It is unbiblical for anyone to say, 'Just believe.'"[2] Our physician, Luke, is giving Theophilus more than an elementary "just believe."

5. *This Book has an unequaled unity from start to finish.* I really like this one. The book we call the Bible has 66 different letters or books, written by 40 different authors from all kinds of walks of life. There are fishermen, highly educated people, political figures, betrayers, humble, and arrogant. The writers are all over the place. The entire Bible, front to back, was written over a span of 1,600 years on three continents in three different languages. Yet it has the stunning unity of paradise lost in the first book to

paradise found in the last book. Now THAT is just plain cool.

6. *Geographical accuracy is found in the Bible.*

7. *Historical accuracy in the Bible is based on archaeology.* There's nothing like a good archaeological dig to substantiate things. People dig around where I live all the time. Kennesaw Mountain is a veritable Civil War history book waiting to be uncovered with each relic found. Haven't you dug up an old something in your backyard, and wondered about the story attached? The grand narrative of scripture has motivated people to dig for years. Inquisitive people have unearthed some real gems, and they point to the accuracy of a very detailed God.

8. *The whole Thing was endorsed by Jesus.* This was probably the best point of my wifeless date night. Without this one, we're right back to religion that leaves us wanting more. All apologetics and Biblical defenses are useful only if they point us to Jesus. Without Jesus, our heads are never connected to our hearts. Too many Christians are dying of this terminal brain disease. Jesus prevents such horrific malady because He not only believed in and used the Bible, He IS the Bible. He IS the Word (John 1:1). He IS the story.

Jacobian's eight points would have made for a horrific date with Sherry. However, they did seem to shield my heart with a wonderful layer of Biblical certainty. Perhaps gaining confidence is what good apologetics are supposed to do. Apologizing for your apologetics because you thumped someone on the head with your twenty-pound King James approach rarely works.

Do you have a certainty of the Bible, which is self-defined as living and active dynamite? Do you have a certainty of your faith and Jesus? Would you like to? Are you tired of the fog and confusion that defines so many people's spiritual lives? Maybe our once-pregnant word *Christian* has lessened because our sacred certainty has too. Our confusion is a hurdle we must try to jump.

There are a lot of things that confuse me these days. I went to my son's soccer practice on a muggy, uneventful Tuesday. There were several teams practicing. I was drawn to an obviously struggling team to the right of my beach chair perch. They were having trouble with unruly little five-year-olds. FIVE-YEAR OLDS. I just happened to note the determined techniques of the coach. At one point the weary coach yelled, "We did not come here to play!" I've been around the motivational speech block a few times, but that one confused me. If you're a five-year-old, that's exactly why you came! You gave up Sponge Bob and you came to play! I was confused by this whole shining moment in toddler sports history.

An Iranian president spoke in New York City recently at Colombia University. I'm not normally politically outspoken, but inviting the leader of a country threatening nuclear war to speak openly at a college positioned in a major U.S. city confused me. My certainty of what the Constitution says about free speech was rattled. To add further insult to my doubting injury, someone asked the opportunistic

Iranian leader if there were any homosexuals in Iran. He said, "No." Was that because there are no homosexuals in Iran or because apparently, if you are a homosexual in Iran, you will be killed? I was confused. Apparently, in Iran, there are no homosexuals. Apparently if you are a homosexual, you will be killed in Iran. I was, apparently, perplexed. Uncertain.

I can go on and on with the stuff of life causing my tumultuous ocean of uncertainty. It's almost laughable how many folks surrounding me look for my pastoral spin to bandage their perplexities. One of life's most baffling puzzlements though is how reasonable, logical, educated, street-wise earthlings can take the weight of evidence concerning the Bible, dismiss Jesus and glibly say, "This is just a concocted thing of bedtime stories. It's just all an enigmatic fluke." (I do like the word "enigmatic" though.)

Where's the needle on your certainty of faith gauge? Can you offer a compelling conversation about Jesus to your neighbor at the next cookout or over the backyard fence? Would you like to? Is it important that I am able to persuade and convince someone of a spiritual peanut butter and jelly sandwich? (Getting tired of that metaphor yet?) There's another Bible writer named Peter who thought that if we set apart Jesus as Lord and actually wear the name of Christian correctly, having a prepared answer for your spiritual hope is important (I Peter 3:15). Jesus followers are supposed to be able to do this. Dr. Luke is willing to help.

Here's one last thought as we quit being Christians and start following Jesus. It's actually a question I fear will put you smack dab back in the middle of the dreaded glaze thing. How did Luke go about writing his book? It's more of a gripping question than you're current yawn would admit. Let's go a bit further...

Most contemporary students of the ancient Dr. Luke believe he used outside sources to write his very detailed and time-tested challenges. One of his primary sources was the gospel letter of Mark. Let me show you why I think this is something incredibly cool to mull over.

If you go into the New Testament book of Mark, there seems to be an obvious absence of excitement or pastor-sanctioned embellishment. Mark 16:6 is a great example. He's writing about the death and resurrection, but without flowery or legendary language. Do you see this? There is to some degree, a serious lack of literary excitement. Hmmm. It's eye-opening to read how many other commentators believe this lack of emotional semantics is what makes Mark a very credible and believable writer. As you move from the resurrection and move hundreds of years into the second and third century, you start to read some very tall, legendary language about that same resurrection. There are documents in the second and third century that, when talking about the death and resurrection of Jesus, have a giant speaking cross with brilliantly staged lights and thousands of beaming angels. The further away you get from the event, the more spectacular the language becomes.

Mark writes, "He died, and He was raised from the dead." Period. Boom. There you go. Deal with it. Umph. Mark, more than likely, wrote within 20 years after the resurrection of Jesus. Are you with me on all of this? Do you understand why this is so very cool? The book of Mark is incredibly credible, and just so happens to be one of the primary sources of Dr. Luke's non-Jewish investigation.

Does this really matter? Are these ideas actually pertinent to our following Jesus, or do they just make me look good as a writer and fill some lonely pages of my book?

If you're able to hold a Bible in your hands --- leather, imitation vinyl, or otherwise --- it's important to know how this living, organic document is also supported by other sources. Some 24,000 other documents, copies, and sources support the credibility of the Bible. Did you know that? 24,000 outside sources support that dusty thing of dynamite perched on your coffee table.

There are historical documents and works of antiquity like Plato, which nobody dares argue. When was the last time you heard someone on Fox News argue Plato? Why aren't there people on the afternoon talk shows saying, "We should defend Plato?" Because it's a fact, Jack. We take that and run with it. Guess how many documents back up and give credibility to Plato? Seven. What about Homer's *Iliad* (now that mention should garner me an honorary degree from somewhere)? Try 643. Not bad, Homer. Doh!

You want certainty? Soak on how important a butt load of outside sources are for our faith and the credibility of the amazing and spectacular Bible. (Yes Church Lady, I just said, "butt load.") And yet, with some 24,000 documents, manuscripts, and copies to give ridiculous credibility, the Bible still remains one of the most attacked and argued compilations out there.

Dr. Luke also tells us he used eyewitnesses to help strengthen his friend Theophilus. Because the New Testament was originally written in Greek, a look at the word "eyewitness" becomes enlightening. In the second verse of Luke's first chapter, he uses the Greek word "autoptes" or "eyewitnesses." Again, you're going to be so smokin' at that next Bible trivia party. Guess what English word comes from "autoptes?" Our happy-snappy word "autopsy" is the correct answer. What happens at a good, old-fashioned autopsy besides the little known and strange dance of the undertaker? There is a detailed, meticulous examination of the facts by a DOCTOR. Did anything just click for you? Did a proverbial light just click on inches above your head?

Dr. Luke wants us to know he's done a detailed examination of the facts, and he's gotten credible eyewitnesses to back it all up. You may ask, "Who were the witnesses?" Well how about Jesus's own mother. Hello? There's a woman who would have known pretty much everything. What about Jesus's brothers? Undoubtedly the Apostles would have been interviewed by our hard-working Dr. Luke. These were guys who lived and traveled with Jesus, saw miracles, and heard unbelievable teaching.

Eyewitness accounts were important in the first century, and still are today. Next time you're in a questionable fender bender, do you want an eyewitness account of what happened? If you're in a courtroom and need a legal defense, the eyewitnesses your lawyer sequesters could potentially determine your fate. For the first-grader whose face just received a punch from an evil older sister, a credible eyewitness becomes money for the verdict rendered by skeptical parents.

After Jesus resurrected, He hung out with good friends for about 40 days. He did that for eyewitness accounts. He did that so we wouldn't have unreasonable blind leaps of faith in making our PB & J sandwich. Jesus wanted us to have a certainty attached to our label of *Christian*. He afforded us the ability to have a reasonable explanation through the detailed autopsy of the facts by a whiz doctor named Luke. It's part of the sheer beauty and amazement of the Bible, and it wonderfully points to Jesus.

There's a great, little verse found in II Timothy 3:16. It's actually a very controversial nugget because of the penetrating first word *all*. That's a powerful word, and it ticks a lot of people off. Some people can believe some of the Bible, but everyone usually does not accept all. However, ALL Scripture is God-breathed. All of the Bible is God-inspired. The entirety can be used for things like teaching, getting in someone's grill for all the right reasons, re-directing, and training in everything pertaining to Jesus.

Luke used outside sources, eyewitness, and detailed accounts to write every word. This does not mean God put certain people into mysterious trances, and blindly guided their hand across the page in order for the Bible to be written. That's just not how we got the Bible, but that's how many people understand, "All scripture is God-breathed."

Here's how it happened with Dr. Luke. God used a smart, intellectual, well-trained man. God selected someone with fortitude and character, who would stick to a critical investigation of the facts. God chose Luke because along with some help by the Holy Spirit (John 14:26), Luke would do the necessary work to write his contributions to the Word of God. This points to the real meaning of God-breathed.

Do you know what you should be asking yourself right now? By the time you get to this particular paragraph, you should be getting a bit fidgety. Here's what you should say out loud even if someone is in the room: "What is the big-honkin' fat deal here?"

Here it is. There are a lot of people these days that are looking for a second opinion. Our once crystallized word *Christian* has become murky and has leaked significance and rally power. Because of that, people these days want second opinions on God, second opinions on Jesus, second opinions on the Bible, and second opinions on spirituality. Second opinions come very cheaply these days.

A while back, a book called *The Secret*, by Rhonda Byrne, hit the retail bookshelves with a vengeance. With the help of people like Oprah, this book was wildly popular. At one point, even Harry Potter couldn't outsell *The Secret.* In my own condensed translation, Rhonda Byrne writes, "You can have, do, and be anything you want through your own power. Just think it. You can do it because you are god." This was the essence of a book that made Rhonda Byrne a very rich woman.

So many people jumped all over this published wonder, even those claiming the name "Christian." As the details of *The Secret* became public, I thought to myself: *"Isn't this like the same old lie Satan used on Eve back in the garden when he said, 'You can become like God'? This is the same thing, only repackaged." The Secret* was the prosperity gospel without Jesus. Wow. That's good news with the good left out. Uncertain seekers were devouring this up because they were looking for a second spiritual opinion. Second opinions fly at people these days with great regularity. Books like *The Davinci Code, The God Delusion,* and *The Secret* are proving to be untested, gullible, best-selling, cheap second opinions.

Are you starting to understand why Dr. Luke can and needs to help us? Ravi Zacharias says, "For all practical purposes truth has been relegated to technology, beauty has been subjugated to the beholder, and goodness is mocked night after night as millions are idiotized before a box."[3] I hope you can see why it's absolutely past time for us to leave confusing labels of *Christian* behind so we can follow Jesus.

Scattered throughout internet blogs are the words of Carl Henry: "We are intellectually uncapped, morally unzippered, and volitionally uncurbed."[4] It seems the masses have carelessly placed the pursuit of truth in the dumper. Jesus said He WAS the truth (John 14:6). Our intentional attempts to follow Jesus are important for our credibility. Our ability to give a reasonable answer for our faith in Jesus, our ability to talk about Him, and the authentic banner we fly is all at stake here.

A couple of weeks ago we had an untagged, unlicensed bulldog show up at our house. We live in Georgia, so a bulldog is not something people just lose or throw away... unless, of course, they went to Georgia Tech. My pet-starved kids immediately said, "He's ours!" For years I've tried to avoid having a dog, and now God placed a freebie on my back porch. I was mad at God. We named him Petey, but Stinky would have been more appropriate. This saggy-faced pup smelled so bad that in order for my kids to keep this stray act of God's wrath on my life, they had to give Petey a bath. They tried, but Petey didn't want a bath. His natural and animalistic inclination was not to be cleansed of his odorous reputation. Once the grimy ruts of his tarnished face were cotton swabbed, we enjoyed the mutt so much more. I think, in the end, Petey probably appreciated it as well.

In order for you and me to quit being Christians to follow Jesus, some washing will be required. When was the last time you were washed by the Word (Eph. 5:26)? It may not be our natural inclination. We may even fight it like a crazed bulldog. Do you need a good bath? Do you need to be washed with water through the Word? I get extremely dirty every week on movies and TV and Internet and magazines and newspapers. My thought life, exposure to off-color jokes and innuendos, pride, and pursuit of stuff just gets me really dirty. I need regular baths.

My tendency, like my youngest son, Michael, is to say, "I don't need a bath." Some of the necessary cleansing from Dr. Luke will prompt many to bolt like a wet canine. But if we stick with this thing, we'll have a revived certainty of faith. Maybe we'll even start to reclaim the power of *Christian* as we follow Jesus. At the very least, we'll make a mean PB & J for our hungry friends.

Chapter End Notes

1. Carl Sagan (writer/host) (December 14, 1980). "Encyclopedia Galactica". Cosmos. episode 12. 01:24 minutes in. PBS.

2. Francis Schaeffer, "The God Who is There" in Trilogy (Wheaton, IL: Crossway Books, 1990), 189.

3. Ravi Zacharias, RZIM, ""Biblical Authority And Cultural Relativism",
http://www.rzim.org/justthinkingfv/tabid/602/articleid/6558/cbm oduleid/881/default.aspx

4. Carl F H Henry, RZIM, "Generations, Regeneration, and the Word",
http://www.rzim.org/usa/usfv/tabid/436/articleid/10197/cbmodule id/1133/default.aspx

Chapter Two

Jesus Glasses

Strategy #2: Begin living expectantly.

Luke 2:21-38

"On the eighth day, when it was time to circumcise him, he was named Jesus, the name the angel had given him before he had been conceived. When the time of their purification according to the Law of Moses had been completed, Joseph and Mary took him to Jerusalem to present him to the Lord (as it is written in the Law of the Lord, "Every firstborn male is to be consecrated to the Lord"), and to offer a sacrifice in keeping with what is said in the Law of the Lord: "a pair of doves or two young pigeons."

Now there was a man in Jerusalem called Simeon, who was righteous and devout. He was waiting for the consolation of Israel, and the Holy Spirit was upon him. It had been revealed to him by the Holy Spirit that he would not die before he had seen the Lord's Christ. Moved by the Spirit, he went into the temple courts. When the parents brought in the child Jesus to do for him what the custom of the Law required, Simeon took him in his arms and praised God, saying: "Sovereign Lord, as you have promised, you now dismiss your servant in peace. For my eyes have seen your salvation, which you have prepared in the sight of all people, a light for revelation to the Gentiles and for glory to your people Israel." The child's father and mother marveled at what was said about him. Then Simeon blessed them and said to Mary, his mother: "This child is destined to cause the falling and rising of many in Israel, and to be a sign that will be spoken against, so that the thoughts of many hearts will be revealed. And a sword will pierce your own soul too." There was also a prophetess, Anna, the daughter of Phanuel, of the tribe of Asher. She was very old; she had lived with her husband seven years after her marriage, and then was a widow until she was eighty-four. She never left the temple but worshiped night and day, fasting and praying. Coming up to them at that very moment, she gave thanks to God and spoke about the child to all who were looking forward to the redemption of Jerusalem."

Has your favorite pastor ever taken time off to fast, pray, and seek God's direction? If so, what was the first sermon like upon their return? Long? Hard? Fiery? Preachy? Did you nudge the person next to you and say, "Give it a few weeks; his fire will die back down." I have found my time away to pray and fast as necessary as my time behind the desk and podium. When I do come back down from my mountaintop, I tend to let'er rip with a "drink from the fire hose" approach. I wrote this chapter after an intentional time away with God. I would apologize for being a bit preachy, but your determination to reclaim the lost power of *Christian* demands you sit and take it like a good Sunday morning congregant. Did I really just use the word "congregant?" I do apologize for that!

As a man of great detail, Dr. Luke takes several eye-opening experiences and writes about the idea of waiting. Dr. Luke writes in his first chapter of Acts how Jesus commanded His followers to, "...not leave Jerusalem, but wait..." (Acts 1:4). Jesus has finished His earthly mission. He's about to ascend to His heavenly position of being a new high priest. Jesus is outta here. He's ready to hand over the Kingdom keys to His mentees. His to-do list of action items has "wait" as the first box to check. Sit and wait. Personally, I find this directive extremely frustrating. Jesus tells His friends to wait for the gift promised by His Father. He is referring to the Holy Spirit, but the idea of waiting takes precedence.

I hate to wait. I can't wait for this book to be done. Whether it's for a convenient pump at a cheap gas station, or a quick lane at the Walmart check-out lines, I don't wait well. My drive for the immediate is a sad reality, and paints the color ugly on the inside of my jacked up heart. Waiting is for the weak who have nothing better to do, right? I couldn't wait for my kids to grow and stand on their own two feet, but now I suddenly have graduating teens. I find myself on the constant verge of tears as a hurried season of life undergoes big change. Idiot! I should have waited.

The Greek word Luke likes to use for waiting is *prosdechomai*. The meaning here is different than my idea of waiting. It's what an old, grey-haired man of faith is doing in the temple at the time of Jesus' birth. He'd been prosdechomai-ing for years. He is waiting for the future. Simeon is waiting forwardly. There is a future worth waiting on, and this Bible enigma is lingering with purpose. Simeon was a New Testament, Godly man expecting Old Testament hopes and promises to be fulfilled. He expected the Messiah. He expected the consolation of God's people. He was wearing his Jesus glasses.

There's a sense of waiting for a better future with *prosdechomai*. Attached to this fun-to-say word is also the sense of waiting actively now. Max Lucado writes how many Christians get consumed with the return of Christ. "Many are into the not yet and forget the right now."[1] I wish I had the patience to write something great like that. You can't be so into the not yet that you miss the right now. That's the point Dr. Luke is trying to get across. I wish my thick skull had absorbed this truth when my now teenage daughters were waking us up for their 2 a.m. feeding. Sit, wait, but enjoy.

Eight days after Jesus was born, it was time for the Jewish ceremony of circumcision. When this special time of spiritual purification came, Jesus' mom and dad took Him to the temple for this strange but necessary event. Do I need to camp out on the physical act of circumcision? Once on a Sunday morning, I tried to explain circumcision by using pruning sheers to creatively display the obvious ouch. A family left our church claiming I crossed lines that shouldn't be crossed on a Sunday morning. The Lord's Day should be kept somewhat sterile and safe for the whole family, right? Whatever. I think this would mean much of the Bible should be left untouched as well. (Have you read the one about the king who cut off several dudes' robes so their bottoms were, well… uhm, butt naked?)

Are you OK with the reality of circumcision? If no explanation is needed, let's move on to the offering Joseph and Mary gave at the time of Jesus' pruning. A pair of doves or pigeons was required. Why is this detail necessary to know? Why did a doctor trained to investigate minute details tell us this? How will this impact my faith and improve my status as *Christian*?

This sounds a lot like my daughter, Lauren, who struggles with how ancient poetic literature will ever play into her potential career choices. You've said this before too, "How am I ever going to use this stuff in my life?" Wait on it.

The Old Testament book of Leviticus gives us clues to explore. In chapter 12, Moses writes about the Jewish traditions attached to birth and circumcision. Dr. Luke subtly points backwards to such traditions to make the reality of Jesus even more so. In Dr. Luke and Theophilus' day, people were seeing the Jesus buzz as all hype. Jesus was seen as a manufactured fraud. In some people's minds, He was definitely not the expected Messiah. This rang true especially for Jewish leaders like the Pharisees, Sadducees, and high priests.

Luke is using traditional details to shout the authenticity of Jesus. Dr. Luke's first intended reader, Theophilus, was Roman. He was a leader in the ever-expanding Roman empire. There was rebellious chatter connected with Jesus on both Roman and Jewish sides of the ancient coin. Theophilus would have every right to drift and question what he actually believed about Jesus.

With details, which initially seem tedious and unimportant, Dr. Luke is proving Jesus is not to be written off. He is not a poser. He is not an insurrectionist. He was raised as a very good Jewish boy in a very real and strict Jewish family. These details slowly gave credibility to Theophilus' new and green faith. It should do exactly the same for us.

There is also something else happening around the time of Jesus' circumcision. Do you see all the old people? Simeon is an old guy, and then there is the appearance of a woman named Anna. Most people think she was a distinguished woman of approximately 105 years old. Her birthday cake would have sent Smokey the Bear into shock. Her wrinkles would have been counted like rings of a fat tree stump. Dr. Luke also includes old people like Elizabeth and Zechariah within the birthing story of the Messiah. Zechariah was a spry 99-year-old with a smoking hot wife of 89. It's not that old people shouldn't take up space in God's Word, but don't you think the comparison to Jesus' parents is striking? Mother Mary was a mere 13 when contractions were five minutes apart.

John Piper says something very interesting about Luke's use of old people. Piper suggests the gospel writer uses four old people surrounding the birth of Christ to say there is a smooth transition between Old Testament and New Testaments.[2] What if old people were purposefully used to signal a change of Old Testament and New Testament guard? Could the old

Jewish ways and traditions be bridged here with the new wine of Jesus? A real guy like Theophilus struggled with believing strong, negative rumors regarding Jesus. A friendly but succinct Luke says, "Don't' go there. Even these older people, who were strict adherents to Old Testament, Jewish ways, were embracing Jesus." You and I can too. We can live and see things through Jesus glasses with great, detailed, and even historical confidence.

An age-defying guy like Simeon is waiting expectantly and actively for his nation of Israel to be comforted. God's people had been in Babylonian slavery because of sin. Ungrateful living after their liberation caused God to be eerily silent for 400 years. Living for a God who took a 400-year vow of silence was tough. Along with the deafening sound of eternal silence, the Romans were kicking the political butts of God's people. Massive Roman power oppressed the Jews back into a form of slavery once again. No wonder Simeon is known for his prosdechomai. Unlike others, Simeon believes things will turn around.

Do you think things can turn around in your life? Are you hoping they will? Hold onto that thought and hope. Surrounding you are people who have stopped hoping. They're called fatalists. How's that for a catchy title on your business card? It's approaching life as Eeyore. "I am who I am. Nothing's gonna change. Everything's probably gonna get worse. My wife is who she is. My kids are just my kids. My job is just my job. The world is going to hell in a seductively woven hand basket. It is what it is." THAT is fatalism. Some people live their lives with a completely opposite mindset of the silver-headed Simeon.

What do you believe? Can Jesus show up in your circumstances, or are you just hoping and waiting for Jesus' second coming because life will be pretty much screwed up until then?

I took a quick look at my Yahoo newsgroup today. Turkey was starting a new and re-energized protest against the United States. They were rioting. The American ambassadors had to pull out of Turkey. Oil soared to a high of $106 a barrel and was climbing at a panicked rate. Four high schoolers were killed in Cleveland. Britney Spears wanted more visitation rights with her kids (imagine their dysfunctional world). Many take a peek at current events and claim it's just the way it is and, in fact, it will probably get worse.

Simeon is a man of God who allows God's Spirit to lead, and he expects to receive something that will turn around everybody's difficult life in Israel, TODAY. Are you able to wait like that?

Couples stream into my office with marriages sadly broken. As they sit gloomy-faced across from me, I try to determine if they believe or even want things to get better. More often than not, I give my pastoral prescription of Ezekiel 36:26. *"I will give you a new heart and put a new spirit in you; I will remove from you your heart of stone and give you a heart of flesh."* I tell the husband to memorize the scripture, put it on the bathroom mirror, and stick it to the visor of his car with a 3x5 card. He needs to pray this verse for his wife. My instructions are to pray for the wife's new spirit, and for her stony heart to be pliable flesh once again. I ask the wife to do the same thing for her husband. With every ounce of pastoral energy I can muster, I ask them to expect God's hand to affect and correct their brokenness. I want them to wait and expect things to change. Prosdechomai.

Other hurting marriages come my way, and two people who once were one begin taking the Eeyore approach. They believe it's not going to get any better, and so they want out. These are always feeling-based decisions. Usually such tired couples become self-fulfilling prophets who have removed their Jesus glasses.

Do you understand the importance of Dr. Luke's detail of waiting expectantly? Your job, finances, spouse, addictions, single-ness, kids, and screwed up church are not viewed as lost causes in the eyes of Jesus. His living and active Word is still the greatest change agent available. Why wouldn't we grow old living expectantly?

Global injustices can still be reversed. There's a global AIDS pandemic affecting the planet, but nowhere seen more than throughout Africa. I've witnessed the effects of AIDS first hand in desperate, widowed, and orphaned Kenyan huts. Millions are dying while other comfortable millions sit lazily and moan, "There's not much you can do about that." We can affect change if we live expectantly of what Jesus wants to do through us. We can if we put on our expectant Jesus glasses.

Remember what happened in Rwanda in 1994? In a furious 100-day stretch, over 800,000 people were slaughtered. Neighbors killed neighbors as tribal differences boiled to murderous levels. The bloody mess initially went under the radar of the selective media in the United States. When it finally came into American awareness, most people, including Christians, coldly believed, "There's not much we can do about that. It's such a shame." In reality, there probably wasn't much any of us could do… unless we did a little prosdechomai-ing ourselves in waiting for the consolation of Rwanda.

There's a group of real-deal Christians who believe Jesus' light can be seen in dark places like Rwanda. They expect a war-torn nation to heal and be restored. These entrepreneurial Jesus followers started a visionary company called "Land of a Thousand Hills Coffee." Having discovered Rwandan coffee beans are really good, the question begged if exporting to the United States could create a God-like movement. What if people started drinking Rwandan coffee and jobs were created to help rebuild lives? Here's the best part. LTHC launched their labor of love and began seeing people who were once killing each other, now working side-by-side picking and washing coffee beans. Land of a Thousand Hills Coffee champions this simple motto: Drink Coffee. Do Good.

Still though, what CAN you and I do? If you can't expectantly start an incredible company like LTHC, the least you can do is expectantly buy and drink their coffee! That's what our church did.

Though the coffee cost a bit more, there's also more purpose. It seems to taste better because of that. With minimal effort, our church decided to help Jesus go into Rwanda to redeem and unite these awesome people. Expectantly we drink coffee so that Jesus can do some incredible good. This is the absolute minimal we can do. What will living expectantly look like in your life?

My mom is an active image bearer of Jesus. Growing up, she took my brother, sister, and me to an orphanage during Christmas. We went to a particular one in Grundy, Virginia. The Grundy Mountain Mission School housed some of the most goose-bumpy, horrific stories you could encounter... especially at Christmas time. There were hundreds of hopeful orphans taking refuge at the Mountain Mission School. As we ventured into their chaotic cafeteria, you could inaudibly hear what hallow eyes were saying. "Pick me. Pick me." They wanted to go home for the holidays, and they didn't know or care where home was. They lived day to day very expectantly for what could happen and make an impact on their future. Those orphaned eyes never stopped hoping things would turn around, even living in an overcrowded institution in one of Virginia's poorest counties.

Do we have those kinds of eyes? Do you believe Jesus will enter your inner moaning for a changed future? How can we live this expectantly? Let's keep going...

Simeon knew his Old Testament and Torah like the back of his age-spotted hand. He was viewed by others as righteous and Godly. He was a worshiper. He feared and revered God. Simeon had something revealed to him by the Holy Spirit. Don't miss this powerful nugget with your impressive speed-reading. Simeon lived life at such a pace that he could actually hear the whispered breath of God's Spirit. The same is true for us. To hear from God, we have to figure out a way to slow down and be still. Simeon was a man of practical spiritual disciplines. He knew the unpopular practice of solitude. He could slow down enough to not only listen, but be moved by the Spirit.

There is something with the Holy Spirit's attempt at moving me which looks nothing like Simeon's experience. I've had far too many opportunities where God speaks, but I offer no visible movement. Have you ever had a prompting from God, but took things only as far as a second opinion from people around you? No movement. God said go, but you analyzed. Then you became paralyzed. Eventually you said "wrong size" and a regrettable "no."

Simeon has every right to just sit tight. He is old, for crying out loud. He is nonetheless moved and ventures into the Temple. Good thing too, because that's when Jesus's parents bring their bundle of messianic joy in for His little operation. Simeon takes the baby Jesus into his prosdechomai arms and proceeds to worship. This is a guy who knows how to wait expectantly no matter the circumstances. It is how he walks with God. It is his spiritual discipline. Simeon is led and prompted by God's Holy Spirit. Notice what Dr. Luke doesn't say about Simeon. He doesn't write anything about Simeon's position. He doesn't mention anything about his power. There are no flowery words about his title. It's almost as if Dr. Luke is telling us, "The one thing that really mattered for this man who lives expectantly was his Spirit-led walk with God." Does living expectantly and being controlled by the Holy Spirit somehow go hand in hand?

The Bible says, *"God's Spirit touches our spirits and confirms who we really are."* (Romans 8:16) If we know who God is, and we know we're His children, then we know we're going to get what's coming to us. Jesus now and Jesus later. Blessings today and inheritance later. How do we know that? Check out this verse: *"No one's ever seen or heard anything like this, never so much as imagined anything quite like it, what God has arranged for those who love him. But you've seen and you've heard it because God by his Spirit has brought it all out into the open before you."* (I Corinthians 2:6) We can live expectantly through the Holy Spirit. Oh, shoot... the Holy Spirit. Dang. We usually mess this whole Holy Spirit stuff up, don't we?

I grew up in a great church where, if the Holy Spirit was mentioned, "IT" was referred to as the Holy Ghost. As a kid, that always seemed strange to me. Actually we never camped out much on the topic of the Holy Ghost. Perhaps it probably would have freaked out too many if we had. There are other people, however, in other great churches who talk about the Holy Spirit a lot. Charismatic, Pentecostal gatherings get quite excited and animated when it comes to the Holy Spirit. Growing up, my church team thought their church team was a little crazy and often associated them with evil pew jumping, snake handlin', and tongues speaking. We certainly didn't want to be like THAT!

I love my home church. They gave me a great heritage of faith, but they prevented a better understanding of the person of the Holy Spirit. Yes, the Holy Spirit is a person. Try a simple Bible search of the human attributes attached to the Spirit. You'll find He has hands, feet, eyes, breath, and other person-like qualities. He is not an "it" similar to a Star Wars tainted force. The Holy Spirit is the third person of the mysteriously real trinity: Father, Son, and Spirit. I believe the Holy Spirit is a very practical, reasonable, and powerful person who can take up active residence inside of us. How does this holy person help you to live expectantly? How does this work?

During the mid-90's, interstate I-75 through Atlanta sported several risqué billboards. To get to my office, I drove 45 minutes on I-75 to travel about five miles. If you've ever driven in Atlanta rush hour traffic, you can feel my automotive pain. Invariably I would creep along the highway hoping God would part the cars like He did the Red Sea. He did not, and so I would drive slowly by a huge billboard advertising a local, topless, sports bar. I view myself as a mostly-good pastor even when I'm driving. This particular predicament would always catch me wondering if there were church folk watching me watch the billboard. Consequently and somewhat weirdly, I would drive with a stiff straight glance ahead with not the slightest tilt to the side. I was not going to get sucked into this trashy marketing campaign. Occasionally though, exactly because I'm such a predictable male, I would take a split-second, guilty look. This was, after all, an 80-foot large, scantily clad woman. Quickly, I would turn my head back to center... shaking off my sin with a blink and self-righteous snort. It was at this point I heard from the person of the Holy Spirit living inside of me. There wasn't an audible voice from a pair of heavenly Bose speakers, but the words were just as clear and penetrating. The Holy Spirit spoke up and said, "Alan, is that what you want? Is that really what you want? Would you give up your wife for that? Would you wreck and ruin your kids and your family for her? Alan, where do you think that smiling, scantily clad, 80-foot large woman is this morning? She's smiling in the air-brushed picture, but is she still happy this morning?" In one last divine moment of teaching, the Spirit asked, "And Alan, do you understand she is somebody's daughter?" I have three girls of my own, so that question hit home. Amazing, isn't it, how a good friend knows just what to say?

I whole-heartedly believe the Holy Spirit convinced me to not lower expectations to levels impossible to be met anyway. The Holy Spirit was helping me live expectantly for Jesus now and towards His second coming. That's how the Holy Spirit works very practically. By the way, He's the kind of person who also likes to give great, personal gifts like love, joy, peace, patience, kindness, goodness, gentleness, faithfulness, and self-control. He gives everything my wife, Sherry, knows I need!

Will you need to adjust your life so that the Spirit can breathe inside you? For me to operate like old Simeon, adjustments seem to be constantly necessary. What about you? A few might initially say, "Give me some of that Spirit," but they also haven't taken the time to know Jesus yet. You need to make Jesus Lord before the Spirit will move fully in.

Sin separates people from God. Jesus died on a rugged cross to build a bridge between God and us. When we accept this bridge of grace, Jesus says, "Now I will fully give you the third person of the trinity to help you and reside inside you." This is how the person of the Holy Spirit moves in and helps us to live expectantly. With the Spirit's personhood pulsing through us, what should we expect to see? What did Simeon see?

Simeon is thought by many to be an old coot off his religious rocker. He is one Passover short of a matzah ball. Because he is always looking for something never there, Simeon's driven-ness makes him look as nutty as that other old guy who built an ark in the desert. How many parents of newborns let a crazy man grab their baby, start singing a song completely out of tune, and mumble some loony phrases? That's exactly what Simeon did with God wrapped in a blanket.

When Sherry and I had Brooklynn, our very first child, we were paranoid idiots. Sometimes people would touch and grab our precious bundle, only to freak us into an emergency alcohol sponge bath. These are the very real antics of newborn parents.

Simeon takes the baby Jesus into his arms, praises God, and says, "Now I can die in peace." What's the whole dying thing about? Is that a little Eeyore coming out of Mr. Positive? Nope. Those are words from someone who lives expectantly. The sting of death holds no power. When you really do the prosdechomai thing right, fear and the eventuality of death turn into a pale shade of impotent. This is what's happening with Simeon. He knows he is holding salvation in his grateful hands. He knows this baby is the consolation of Israel. Simeon is holding the long awaited Messiah. The comfort of all nations has arrived. Simeon's life and waiting has now been completed.

I'm not sure this old coot even saw a baby when he was holding a diapered Jesus. This was no ordinary newborn. Shepherds were freaked out by this kid. Asian wise men brought extravagant gifts to Mary's baby shower. King Herod signed a royal edict to have this baby killed. This was a much-ballyhooed child. I don't think Simeon saw any of this baby/child stuff. According to the Bible, these wise, old eyes saw the redemption and restoration of mankind. Simeon lived expectantly, and he saw salvation. If you were to live expectantly, what would you expect to see? Would seeing Jesus be enough, or would you want your shopping list filled? Do you have an agenda? What is it you want to see?

In only my second mission trip outside the United States, I flew into the dark continent of Africa to work in Kenya. I was excited to go, but developed very early expectations of flying back home the day before Thanksgiving. I began expecting hugs from my children I love. Even before climbing aboard the first plane, I was envisioning big, wet, juicy, romantic, reunited kisses from the wife I deeply love. Before setting foot in Kenya, I was already mentally playing out the big family reunion coinciding with turkey and homemade pumpkin pie. Living expectantly with a family I adore enabled me to see all of this before it actually unfolded. If you're living expectantly with Jesus glasses on, what do YOU see?

Can you see salvation for your spouse? In spite of Sunday mornings being a nagging hassle, can you see it? You're begging the other half to go to church with you has been futile for years. Can you expectantly see Jesus turning all of this around? Can you see life-giving restoration for your drifting kids? Maybe they're older and have really gone down a bad track. You don't know what to do any longer. What are you expecting to see? What can you see with your Jesus glasses on?

Simeon doesn't seem as crazy to us as he did to his ancient contemporaries. Well, wait a minute. Did you catch what he said after the elation and worship part of the story? He mumbled something about the baby Jesus being, "...destined to cause the falling and rising of many in Israel." Just when you thought the nut farm had been closed, Simeon says something equivalent to, "Your baby is ugly!" Try that little nursery axiom the next time you're in the baby wing of a hospital. Simeon made a prophetic proclamation.

The Jesus baby was going to really stir things up. This infant would cause trouble. There would be no neutral ground for people to stand on concerning the Messiah. Jesus, the old man claimed, would not live an easy life for Himself. As inspiring and joyful as Simeon's first words were to Mary, these final ones cut like a rusty surgeon's knife.

With his old, worn, Jesus glasses on, did Simeon see anything that resembles a baby? Did he see a rugged cross instead? He would not live long enough to witness Jesus' crucifixion, but did his expectant eyes see blood and nails? Expectant Jesus glasses aren't necessarily always rose-colored.

Our expectant story includes another old person. Just as Simeon is lifting up the infant personification of God, a woman named Anna grabs the Biblical spotlight. Many want her in the same insane asylum as Simeon. Like her elder counterpart, Anna's bio includes words like strange, crazy, and out of touch. She too lived every day of her lonely widowed life in the temple waiting. Some people think she and Simeon should have hooked up to make the perfect, silver-headed couple. Anna though is focused on one thing and one thing only. Jesus. The Messiah. Redemption. Salvation. Restoration. Eternal hope. People wrote this self-proclaimed prophetess off of their Christmas card list because she was doing more of that annoying prosdechomai. She longs only for Jesus now and Jesus later.

People thought Simeon and Anna were weird. They were classified as spiritual nut jobs in most religious circles. This fact bothered me as I realized nobody paints me into any similar padded corner. I don't view myself as weird, and that bothers me. Would I be stranger if life was lived more expectantly? Would there be less complaining and more loving? Would I offer fewer excuses, but more service? I think I would worship more and maybe sing less. Perhaps my leadership would be less controlling and more inclusive. Expectant living may even drive me to give more and accumulate less. Undoubtedly, this kind of living would be labeled by most as weird. I think that would be cool. Most Christians would likely counsel me to get counseling. My honest confession, though, is this: I don't think I'm strange enough (although my teenage kids would vehemently argue).

I tend to work hard at being a full time pastor, but much less at expectantly living. I don't think teaching in jeans every Sunday morning is enough. It's just not weird enough, no matter how fired up I get. I don't want to lead a boring, comfortable, predictable, mediocre church. These days I daydream the possibilities of an entire church living expectantly for Jesus. Weird, huh? What if a body of believers put their Jesus glasses on and expected a fully transforming salvation? Worship would most definitely be different... better. Church world would be alive, again, with Holy Spirit movements. Someone might even dare to label us as a strange cult. What if local gossip relegated our church as a Jesus cult unlike typical Christians? How cool would that be?

A graciously edgy-but-older man works in the office next to mine. His name is Rob Irvine. He tells me about a season of life when he just didn't care about things like insurance and retirement funds. He believed and lived as if Jesus were coming back. In past years, Rob pushed his life out onto the edge where faith turns your knuckles sparkling white. "Now," Rob bemoans, "I've got a 401K and everything neatly figured out. There was a time when we'd talk about the second coming, work to be done, vitally active faith, intensity and living expectantly. But then," Rob quips, "I got old and safe." Rob is openly bothered by the way most people say life should be lived, and he wants to make necessary adjustments in the other direction.

Wrongly branded Christians need to make a few adjustments too. Rob did, and months after his sobering conversation with me, I heard a completely different perspective from another old coot who decided to put his Jesus glasses back on.

Rob and his wife Judy are empty nesters, but his nearby son challenged Rob to flip a house with him in downtown Atlanta. The market was good, and they stood to make a ton of money. Rob's son, Reed, had developed a plan to buy an old house and renovate it. When asked who's money would be used, Reed confidently replied, "Yours dad!" The response from dad was an immediate "no." The project would require too much money and effort for an old pastor with a cushy retirement plan.

About the time Reed was being rejected, God sent Rob to a conference called "Orange" where he heard Donald Miller speak. Donald Miller is the engaging author of great books like, "Blue Like Jazz." Miller told a story at the conference, and it rocked Rob's world. Apparently a puzzled father spoke with Donald Miller about his daughter who was in trouble with a loser boyfriend, drugs, alcohol, and the whole addictive nine yards. The father did not have the slightest clue as to what went wrong with his daughter. In classic Donald Miller fashion, the push back came. "Maybe it's your fault. Maybe you've not given your daughter enough story." Miller questioned if the dad's version of life was boring. What if the wayward girl needed story that came with living expectantly? What if the daughter was so bored, she went off in other directions searching for skewed adventures instead of Godly ones? What if it was the father's fault? That timely story prompted Rob to pick up the phone and tell his son, "Let's do the house thing... together!" Rob made a great decision to build into his son. He took a severe financial hit, but he created great story with his son. He began to live expectantly. Forwardly. Prosdechomai.

If we apply the lessons of Simeon, it will affect the way we raise our kids. Shame on us, as parents, if our kids are bored and lifeless. It's our problem, not theirs. If we're not living life expectantly, neither will they.

After coming off my week of fasting mentioned earlier, God showed me I wasn't living out the truths of what Simeon's example afforded. Through the lens of Jesus glasses, I saw what needed to be taught, but I also wasn't living. I needed to quit being a safe,

American Christian in order to follow Jesus. Sometimes these necessary God moments wake us to the way life is supposed to be lived. It's a stark juxtaposition of how we're actually living. During those times, we can only pray, "God, I'm sorry. Please help me live with a holy expectation from this day forward. Thanks for rocking my world. Now rock the worlds of those around me."

Slip a pair of Jesus glasses on. What are you able to see?

Chapter End Notes

1. Max Lucado, <u>When Christ Comes</u>, (Word Publishing, 1999), 17.
2. John Piper, Sermon: "<u>Simeon's Farwell To The World</u>", http://www.desiringgod.org/resource-library/sermons/simeons-farewell-to-the-world.

Chapter Three

Glow Sticks In The Blender

Strategy #3: Shape vision with Jesus's mission.

Luke 4:14-21

*"Jesus returned to Galilee in the power of the
Spirit, and news about him spread through the whole
countryside. He taught in their synagogues, and
everyone praised him. He went to Nazareth, where he
had been brought up, and on the Sabbath day he went
into the synagogue, as was his custom. And he stood
up to read. The scroll of the prophet Isaiah was
handed to him. Unrolling it, he found the place where
it is written: "The Spirit of the Lord is on me, because
he has anointed me to preach good news to the poor.
He has sent me to proclaim freedom for the prisoners
and recovery of sight for the blind, to release the
oppressed, to proclaim the year of the Lord's favor."
Then he rolled up the scroll, gave it back to the
attendant and sat down. The eyes of everyone in the
synagogue were fastened on him, and he began by
saying to them, "Today this scripture is fulfilled in
your hearing."*

At a recent gathering of church elders, I
reluctantly pulled my glasses out to read a small font
document. I hate to use my glasses. It's a denial
thing. Even with spectacles, I had to hold the paper at

arm's length. It had been a couple years since my optometrist updated the prescription. One of our smart-alec elders jokingly said, "Do you want me to hold it for you?" Jon Franz, an elder and supposed Godly man, then asked if I wanted to use his glasses. In reality he was asking if I was ready to stop denying my 50-ness. Jon had one of those cheapo pair of magnifying glasses you can score for five bucks at Walgreens. I told Jon and the guys that an off the rack pair of glasses would never work for my sensitive and delicate eyes. Jon pushed them under my nose and pressed me to give them a try. I comically put them on, but then suddenly... boom, I could see. It was amazing. Right there in a holy elder's meeting, the gang busted out laughing at my squinting face. I'm certain these guys will someday answer to a fiery God for their total disrespect of the pastor. After all, why would they laugh at someone going blind right before their eyes? Truth be told, I was laughing right alongside my four-eyed, leader friends.

Eyesight can be a very serious problem. Do you know what Amblyopia is? It's commonly called "lazy eye." One eye is just a little bit lazier and works less than the other. Color blindness is a real condition that keeps a lot of people out of the military. Dry eye syndrome is where eyes can't lubricate themselves. You can't form tears and cry. That would come in handy at my daughter's wedding. Hyperopia is farsightedness. Myopia is nearsightedness. Presbyopia is the fear of seeing Presbyterians. No... actually it's the difficulty to see extremely close up when you're over 40.

This eye stuff can be serious trouble for many of us, especially those of us with "elder" attached in some shape or form to our title. Beyond all the above listed "opias," there is another serious condition of not being able to see things differently than we're used to. I call it Churchyopia. It happens a lot within the walls of buildings we call churches. Not seeing things differently, creatively, freshly, or relationally is a large reason why many have quit going to church. Churchyopia seems to be spreading. Such a malady is why more and more folks want to stop being a stereotypical Christian to follow Jesus.

As a pastor, I want people to see things differently. I want to keep a culture of change and relevance constantly in motion in order to keep God out of our preconceived boxes. One Sunday morning I blended glow sticks in a 10-speed, 800-watt blender. I had seen this done on Youtube, but was betting nobody had ever seen this done in church. Those attending that Sunday definitely saw something different. With the auditorium pitch black, blending glow sticks was a great way to wake people up. I creatively encouraged sleepy minds to see things differently. By the way, I also killed my blender.

I want you to see something differently than perhaps your Churchyopia has allowed. Perhaps you've seen the words of Isaiah 61:1-2 before: *"The Spirit of the sovereign Lord is on me because the Lord has anointed me to preach good news to the poor. He has sent me to bind up the broken hearted, to proclaim freedom for the captives and release from darkness for the prisoners, to proclaim the year of the Lord's favor and the day of vengeance of our God."* Wow. That's some lofty stuff, isn't it? What do those words really mean? What do you see? Let's drop these words into Dr. Luke's 800-watt blender, and see if they will glow brilliantly and differently than expected.

Throughout the New Testament book of Luke, we see Jesus doing the incredible. Miracles, healing, raising people from the dead, casting out demons, calming tsunamis, and feeding the hungry is a part of the normal Kingdom life of Jesus. I look at the resume' of Jesus and say, "Oh snap." It's quite impressive when you begin seeing it all. However, before these really cool accomplishments were unfolding, there's something for us to consider… to see differently.

Jesus is at the Jordan River getting baptized. Yep, He's dunked just like many of us have been. The Holy Spirit descends on Jesus, and He's sent into the desert to wrestle with Satan himself. Jesus did some serious butt whooping on the Adversary's behind. He used the Bible as a weapon of choice. It is written. It is written. It is written. Satan has no defense against Jesus or us when the Bible is used as a double-edged sword.

After the desert battle, Jesus returned to the region of Galilee. Galilee was the home stompin' ground of Jesus. This is where he did life. Jesus walked and moved being powered by the Holy Spirit. In the power of the Spirit he fought Satan, traveled, spoke, taught, and popularity began to spread. He was plugged into His God source.

Now watch this. See something differently. Jesus taught in synagogues and people were asking for autographs. Hmmm. Interesting. Synagogue meetings would be synonymous to our corporate church gatherings. The Jewish people would gather in a synagogue for lots of reasons: weddings, funerals, and any excuse for a meal. Think potluck dinner. A synagogue was very much a Jewish community center. On Saturdays, the Jewish people would gather for worship and teaching. The commoners would sit on the floor in the middle of the synagogue rather informally using dusty mats. There were stone benches around the inside synagogue walls where the important, pious, envied religious people would sit. There was one special seat in the center of the stone benches called the Moses seat. You were really important if you sat there. Like a big shot celebrity sitting courtside with sunglasses at an NBA game, the person nailing down the Moses seat was noticeably distinctive.

A worship service in a synagogue would start with the Shamah... the Old Testament Jewish prayer (Deuteronomy 6:4). "Hear, O Israel, the Lord our God, the Lord is one." For hundreds upon hundreds of years, the Shamah was recited. The Eighteen Benediction prayer would follow. What we know as the Lord's Prayer comes from a portion of the Eighteen Benediction prayer. Then somebody would read out of Torah. Torah is the law, and the first five books of the Old Testament. Genesis, Exodus, Leviticus, Numbers, and Deuteronomy make up Torah. The Jewish people loved Torah. They celebrated, danced with, kissed, memorized, and lived by their much-loved Torah.

After an anticipated and satisfying drink from Torah, another person would read an assigned portion of scripture from one of the Old Testament prophets... like Isaiah. This reading from the prophets was planned months in advance like many lectionary readings. The reader of the prophets would also be the one to sit in the Moses seat. Can you imagine the pressure attached to that assignment? All eyes would be on the reader who sat prominently in the hallowed Moses seat. You know this guy would be sweating bullets. Do you think anyone who sat in the Moses seat ever scratched their initials in the stone bench, or wrote: "Fred wuz here?" Nah, probably not.

All of this is a small slice of what happened in a Jewish synagogue on any given ancient Saturday. Like religious clockwork, this was what most traditional Jewish people did. With these details in mind, open up your eyes and see what happened.

Jesus goes into Nazareth, a small town in Galilee, on a Sabbath Saturday and rolls into a synagogue. Nazareth is the town Jesus grew up in. Nazareth is a village that carried a few nicknames like: Messiah-town or Messiah-ville. Everyone in Nazareth is Messiah crazy. This burgeoning city is a hot bed of people who actively believe and articulate, "The Messiah's coming, The Messiah's coming!" The Jewish people had been waiting for hundreds of years for the Messiah. If you are a good, married Jewish girl and you're pregnant, you could be having the Messiah. People get very excited about your special glow. That is the prevalent thinking. A palpable anxiousness permeates the streets and conversations in Nazareth. If you are a bad Jewish girl who has come up unmarried and pregnant, you are considered a threat to the Messiah. Extremely harsh treatment follows any woman who is carrying an illegitimate baby. That baby, the Jewish people say, is a "mamzer." A mamzer is the equivalent of our very crude slang of "bastard." A mamzer is not allowed to go into the synagogue. A mamzer is not allowed to play with the other Jewish kids. A mamzer is openly ostracized. The mother of a mamzer is also shunned like a Krispy Kreme manager at an LA Fitness Center.

Are you seeing things differently yet? Mary is the mother of a mamzer. This is why there was no room in the inn for Mary and Joseph when they went to Bethlehem. You remember that whole story, don't you? Does this give you a bit different perspective? Mary and Joseph knock on the door of a motel, so we think, but all they get is a neon flashing sign that says "no vacancy." The hard truth points away from an idealized motel, and instead to a family dwelling where many relatives of Mary and/or Joseph were staying.

Jewish people never turn anybody away --- especially not family. Jewish folks are the most hospitable people on the planet. Jewish people to this day pride themselves on their relentless hospitality. Why would Joseph and a teenage pregnant Mary get the cold shoulder from their Jewish family? Mary wasn't married. She was carrying a bastard... a mamzer. Mary and the baby were a threat and an embarrassment to the hopes of a Messiah.

Jesus, as a labeled mamzer, would not have been able to attend the funeral of His earthly father Joseph. Funerals happened in the synagogue. He was barred from going into the synagogue where much of Jewish life was celebrated. We read in the New Testament where Jesus prays, "Abba, Abba, Abba, Abba." Abba means Daddy in Aramaic. We pray lofty prayers that often include a formal, "O Lord our heavenly Father." Jesus prayed "Daddy." Have you ever wondered why He prayed this way? If you were ostracized from life, turned away at your own father's funeral, and whispered about at every turn, wouldn't you need a daddy? Wouldn't your loneliness necessitate a heavenly Father as more of a daddy than an enshrined God? Isn't this our experience as well?

So Jesus grows up, and He comes back to His hometown of Nazareth. See differently the tension that fills the synagogue as Jesus enters. Wow. Can't you see the elbows flying and whispers about the bastard who's not supposed to be here? Now look at the tension that's there as He walks into the synagogue. "Isn't that the mamzer? Isn't that Mary's son? He's never been inside a synagogue. He can't come in here!" Perhaps the whispering turns into vocal complaining. Not only does Jesus stroll into the synagogue, but He stood up and read. Do you SEE this? What did He read? He reads the planned section of scripture from one of the prophets. It's the prophet Isaiah. A messianic prophecy. You gotta admit, that's a pretty wild coincidence considering the passage

Jesus reads on this particular day. Where did He sit then? In the Moses seat? A mamzer can't sit in the Moses seat. Are you kidding me? Like Snoop Dogg sitting at the head table position and saying grace for Thanksgiving dinner with my southern Indiana family, this would be scandalous. At the very least, it would make the local paper. Whoa.

The ancient Jewish people believed there were two very important people, Moses and Elijah. The only person more important was the Messiah. Hmmm. Jesus is sitting in the seat of Moses. He stands up to read. The scroll of the prophet Isaiah is handed to Him. It's already marked with a bulletin and order of worship for this fateful Saturday's service.

Now watch this... see this whole thing unfold differently than perhaps you've seen before. Like other studious Jewish boys, Jesus probably had the entire Old Testament memorized by about the age of 14. The question becomes, did He merely read the prepared scroll, or did He stand up and recite it with great passion and confidence from memory? You want my opinion? I think Jesus presents the planned text and recites it without looking down at the scriptural notes. He's piercing the crowd with His blazing eyes as He speaks the words of Isaiah 61:1-2. It's as if Jesus is dramatically personalizing the text... *"The Spirit of the Lord is on me because he has anointed me to preach good news to the poor. He has sent me to proclaim freedom for the prisoners and recovery of sight for the blind, to release the oppressed, to proclaim the year of the Lord's favor."*

At this point, the Jewish people sitting in that fateful synagogue stop their murmuring in order to wipe drool and suck their tongues back into deathly pale faces. This passage from Isaiah is pointing to the Messiah. In a town nicknamed Messiah-ville, Jesus is announcing that He's it.

Jesus hands the prophecy scroll back to the synagogue attendant and sits down. You know where He sits, right? In the coveted Moses seat. How dare a mamzer do such a thing! How cool that Jesus does. The eyes of the gossip-bent worshipers are stunned and glued on Jesus. He just flashed His Messiah badge, and sat down in the Moses seat. That would make anyone from Messiah Town need a Valium.

There's something else to adjust your bifocals on. Twenty-five years earlier in a little town called Sephoras (a stone's throw away from Nazareth), there was a guy who rose up and said, "I'm the Messiah." He and a band of idiots attempted a revolt against Rome. Rome swooped down and crushed the entire city of Sephoras. Do you suppose any of these gasping folks sitting in the synagogue were saying, "Oh shoot. Here we go again. Rome is going to kick our butts."

No wonder their eyes fastened on Jesus. Just to make things really interesting Jesus informs the reeling crowd that the prophecy from Isaiah has now been fulfilled. He's leaving no doubt. He's the Messiah. Additionally, not only does Jesus clearly communicate who He is, He also establishes the parameters of His mission. Jesus is the self-proclaimed Messiah, and He's beginning His mission of preaching things like:

good news, freedom for the prisoners, sight for the blind, and the year of the Lords favor or Jubilee (we'll get to that one in a sec).

Was Jesus's way of seeing things affected by His mission? Is our ability to see somehow related to our mission? Again, take a look at the mission of Jesus. Preaching salvation and freedom are top priority. The Greek word Jesus uses for "freedom" deals specifically with the debt and weight of sin. Sight for the blind, as Jesus proposes, goes beyond physical blindness. Relief and release for the oppressed points to original Greek language meaning "broken to pieces." Jesus's mission is to focus on broken people. Finally, the very Jewish idea of Jubilee was something also attached to Jesus' mission (again, we'll get to that in just a sec).

Once you understand Jesus's self-proclaimed mission, you begin to understand how He could view people the way He did. For instance, there is this one gal who flat out lied to Jesus --- the embodiment of truth. Oh the audacity. Here's a real piece of work who's had five husbands, and she's sleeping with the next guy in line. Where does Jesus's patience, grace, and love come from when dealing with such capital "L" losers? What keeps Jesus from just slapping a bit of sense into her? One holy whack seems appropriate. There's another sleazy woman literally caught in the act of adultery by religious watchdogs. Yeah, think about that nifty scenario. How DID that happen? Jewish laws dictated that such a low life be quickly destined for a pile of rocks aimed at her head. A public and painful stoning is about all this trouble maker has to look forward to. Why doesn't Jesus throw a rock or two Himself? Where does His restraint come from? Beyond composure, how does love, mercy, and grace flow when it's obvious to everyone what's really needed? Then there's the injustice of the crucifixion. Jesus experiences excruciating pain, and somehow manages to a offer a surprising, "Father, forgive them. They don't know what they're doing." How could He say that?

Jesus knew His mission, and His mission affected His vision of other people. How's your vision these days? How do you see things and people? I'm wondering how other people describe my vision of other people. I wonder about those people I work with. What would they say about Alan's viewpoint and perspective of other people?

What's your opinion of faces flashing across your cable TV news channels? What words come to mind as you scan the infamous list of characters (dead or alive) like Osama Bin Laden, Lindsey Lohan, Amy Winehouse, Tiger Woods, the whole Kardashian family, and the gang on Jersey Shore? What raw response do you have when someone suggests "Snooki" for your baby's name? Do words like evil, troubled, sick, and hopeless idiots come to mind?

What thoughts do we attach to news flashes of convicted sex offenders? We see the pictures often; they're sickos who prey on our kids. Demented is the adjective of choice. Depraved is the proper Biblical term. Who parented such animals? Maybe they should be locked up too!

How does Jesus view such people? How does He see the folks we quickly write off? Remember, His mission was about good news, salvation, prisoners, the weight of sin, the debt of sin, blindness, brokenness, and unhampered love.

Here is your glow stick in a blender moment. Turn the blender on high and see things... people... differently. Wildly, the Bible urges us to have the same attitude as that of Jesus (Philippians 2:5). We're supposed to have the same eyesight and vision for people that Jesus had. Even the messed up people. Especially the messed up people. Jesus tells us how we are sent in the exact same way His Father sent Him (John 17:18). You, me, and Jesus have the same mission. If His mission is our mission, than we should also see the way He sees. THAT is 20/20 vision. Perfect. Holy.

I really like what Leonard Sweet wrote in his book, *The Gospel According to Starbucks*. Sweet simultaneously struck nerves and beautiful chords when he insisted, "The goal of Christianity is not to make us into better people."[1] Initially, like me, you may be a bit confused by that. Give this a little soak time. The goal of Christianity is not to make a better version of you and me. Sweet continues, "The goal of Christianity is not for us to become Christ-like. The goal is for us to be little Christs." That's really good, isn't it? Plant that little gem of a quote on your Facebook status. You'll feel like a better person if you do. Wait, the goal is not for you to become a better person unless that better person is Jesus! Write that on your status update. Jesus is the better person. The touch of Jesus should be my touch. The listening of Jesus should be the way I listen. The voice of Jesus should be the way I speak. And the eyesight and vision of Jesus is the way I'm supposed to see other people.

My two youngest kids afforded me a very rich and funny experience recently at their elementary school. Sherry and I love the kids' school. It's a very culturally challenging and ethnically diverse school. We went to a recent PTA meeting, and there were a lot of Hispanic parents there. I love that. In the chaos of a packed out PTA meeting, one unwitting, very white, very middle-class, extremely suburban female walked to the microphone and announced, "If anybody needs Hispanic translation, just raise your hand." I about busted a cafetorium gut right there in the PTA meeting. My wife was sure I was going to be sent to the principal's office. Sherry couldn't make sense of my squelched laughter. I told her, "If anybody DID need Hispanic translation, how on earth would they understand such a ridiculous announcement?" I thought it was very funny. I tend to crack myself up, especially when survival of a PTA meeting demands some form of childish entertainment.

A couple days later I was pointing a friend to my obvious PTA humor. My friend went off on me. In a breathless rant I was blasted with a, "I'm so tired of these illegal immigrants, and why do WE have to learn Spanish? They should learn English. And we're paying for their health care..." It just went on and on and off in a torrential down pour of hate. I was stunned. My friend also claims to be a Christian. This little tirade made me question the last time I lost it on someone who didn't fit my definition of likeable. When that happens, I've forgotten the mission of Jesus and my vision requires a new prescription.

One last point to blend and let glow. Remember that whole year of the Lord's favor, Jubilee thing? What was this? It was a part of Jesus' mission too. When Jesus talked about proclaiming the year of the Lord's favor, most believe He was pointing to the Old Testament concept of Jubilee. The word *jubilee* in the Hebrew means, "sound the horn." Here's the deal. The Jewish people took a Sabbath and rested every seventh day. They didn't do so much as a smidgen of work. Every seventh year they let their fields rest and didn't plant. Every seventh, seventh year, which is year 49 turning year 50 (did you follow that?) there was a glorious year of Jubilee. That was definitely a time to don a cone-shaped hat and sound the horn.

The concept of Jubilee can be found in Leviticus 25, starting with verse eight. It's worth looking up. Very cool stuff. "Count off seven Sabbaths of years, seven times seven years, so that the seven Sabbaths of years amount to a period of 49 years." (Tell your kids multiplication works even in the Bible!) "Then have the trumpet sounded everywhere on the tenth day of the seventh month on the Day of Atonement, have the trumpet sounded throughout your land. Consecrate the fiftieth year and proclaim liberty throughout the land to all its inhabitants. It shall be a Jubilee - sound the horn - for you. Each one of you is to return to his family property and to each his own clan. The fiftieth year shall be a Jubilee for you. Do not sow and do not reap what grows of itself or harvest the untended vines for it is a Jubilee and it is to be holy for you. Eat only what is taken directly from the fields. In this year of Jubilee everyone is to return to his own property."

In the year of Jubilee you got your land back. If you had sold or hocked your land... your inheritance... you got it all back on Jubilee. Can you imagine this? Thirty years ago I sold my baseball card collection to make some financial ends meet. It was a smokin' collection of about 3,000 cards. I possessed a coveted Topps 1967 Brooks Robinson. In my rubber-banded stacks were a Johnny Bench rookie card, and classic duplicates of Mays, Seaver, and McCovey. Now that I'm collecting baseball cards with my young son, I think often about the cards I used to have. What if twenty more years passed, and suddenly my collection of cards were all given back? That would be a very good day.

In the ancient of days, if you were a poor person and you sold yourself into slavery, you got your freedom back at Jubilee. How do you think that felt? Every fifty years, Jubilee started on the Jewish holiday of the Day of Atonement. This exceptional day allowed God's people to go before the Lord and say, "Forgive me. Wipe out all of my sins." Jubilee set sin, losses, and everything right. I think we all could use a Jubilee.

The average American credit card debt is $9,900. Seems most could use a good Jubilee. Jubilee could be the stuff Presidents get elected for, except you'd have to wait a stinkin' fifty years. Stink.

Often times, ancient kings would come into office, and would garner great loyalty by declaring a year of Jubilee. Kings would set all of the social and economic injustices right. The Jewish people believed that when the Messiah came and sat on his throne, he would usher in a year of Jubilee.

Watch this. Jesus read from the prophets and sat in the Moses seat. He declared His mission of Jubilee to set stuff and people free. Yep. He's definitely pointing to Himself as the long awaited Messiah. But wait; look closer. From Luke chapter 4, Jesus seems to have forgotten something. If Jesus is reading from Isaiah 61:1-2, He seems to have left off that very last phrase of what the prophet was saying... *"and the day of vengeance of our God."* Why did Jesus drop the fire and brimstone thing of vengeance when He spoke in the synagogue?

Here's my best take on this. I believe Jesus is telling us He came the first time to set everything straight. Period. He came the first time to take care of the debt and the weight of sin. Jesus came the first time to take care of spiritual blindness. Jesus was, in essence, saying, "I'm coming this first time to take care of people who are shattered and broken." The first coming of Jesus was to take care of His mission. BUT, the second time He comes, Jesus says, "Vengeance will be unmistakably Mine."

If that is true, Jesus did not come to usher in a year of Jubilee; He came and ushered in an AGE of Jubilee. The age of Jubilee will last until He returns with a vengeance. This is a Billy Graham, amen, the-blender-is-glowing moment. Do you SEE this? Jubilee was a cool idea, but waiting fifty years was a bummer, right? What if we lived in an age of Jubilee -

-- constant and ongoing with every breath you breathe? An age of Jubilee would constantly and continually set captives free. People who deal with the weight and the depth of sin, addictions and pornography, lying and cheating --- would be made right. Everything would be made right by the One sitting in the Moses seat. Whatever imprisons you can be made right. Blow the party horn, dude.

It's the age of Jubilee, and you should have eyes of Jubilee. You and I should see things differently. What if you viewed your spouse through eyes of Jubilee? Your spouse needs good news. Maybe they feel imprisoned, blind, shattered, or broken. I wonder what freedom might do for them? Maybe things just need to be made right. With Jesus this becomes totally possible.

How many parents need to consider offering Jubilee to their teenager? I know I certainly do. Why don't I view my own texting teens as needing good news from me instead of incessant harping, barking, and flexing of parental muscles. Blind, shattered, broken teens are desperate for things to be made right. Jesus can do that as He lives through me. It's His mission. His mission changes how I view things... people... and my kids.

Got a boss whom you wish wasn't? You are so done with that guy... or lady (and that ain't no lady!). Is there anyway you could see them with eyes of Jubilee? That's the way Jesus did it. What if we actually saw people through eyes of amazing grace? We love to sing about it, but do we actually offer grace through eyes of Jubilee?

You might be a bit frustrated that my concern here seems to be so much about others. Someone may be thinking, "There's no way I can focus on someone else when I'm so screwed up myself." Maybe you need to grab onto some Jubilee. Maybe you prayed a prayer years ago to make Jesus your Savior, but the idea of Lord has never taken root. That's one of the problems with our anemic title of Christian. There's a bunch who want to get to heaven, but letting Jesus bring heaven to earth by living fully through us is a whole other story, brutha. Now that you know Jesus' heart, and how He wants to give good news to free and help you see better --- why wouldn't you want Him as Lord? He knows you're shattered and broken. He wants to release you from all that. Jesus wants to set everything right for YOU. Why don't you grab onto some Jubilee?

Are you seeing things differently? Jesus followers do. Christians need to. Let the blenders everywhere begin to glow! Can you imagine if our eyesight was impacted by the mission of Jesus? Can you imagine if Jubilee was offered because Jubilee has also set us free? Wow. If Jesus made things right through us, our PR problem as Christians would be over. To that end, may our mission and perspectives be exactly the same as Jesus' exactly because we no longer live but He lives in us. I can SEE it.

Chapter End Notes

1. Leonard Sweet, <u>The Gospel According to Starbucks</u>, (Colorado Springs, CO: Waterbrook Press 2007) pg. 48-49.

Chapter Four

Miracle Whip

Strategy #4: Adjust your quest for the spectacular.

Luke 4:31-41

"Then he went down to Capernaum, a town in Galilee, and on the Sabbath began to teach the people. They were amazed at his teaching, because his message had authority. In the synagogue there was a man possessed by a demon, an evil spirit. He cried out at the top of his voice, "Ha! What do you want with us, Jesus of Nazareth? Have you come to destroy us? I know who you are—the Holy One of God!" "Be quiet!" Jesus said sternly. "Come out of him!" Then the demon threw the man down before them all and came out without injuring him. All the people were amazed and said to each other, "What is this teaching? With authority and power he gives orders to evil spirits and they come out!" And the news about him spread throughout the surrounding area. Jesus left the synagogue and went to the home of Simon. Now Simon's mother-in-law was suffering from a high fever, and they asked Jesus to help her. So he bent over her and rebuked the fever, and it left her. She got up at once and began to wait on them. When the sun was setting, the people brought to Jesus all who had various kinds of sickness, and laying his hands on each one, he healed them. Moreover, demons came out of many people, shouting, "You are the Son of

God!" But he rebuked them and would not allow them to speak, because they knew he was the Christ."

Any curious white space given at the beginning of this chapter is gratuitous. It's free. Most people don't know this, but you don't actually pay for the extra white space given at chapter breaks. It's a publishing world trade secret. Go ahead. Take it. It's yours. It came with the book, but it's absolutely free. In this great white space, write down a miracle you need. Give it a shot. Scribble something down. It's a nifty little exercise. Your miracle could be relational. It might have to do with your health, your finances, your kids, or your marriage. What is it you need from God right now? At any given moment, don't most of us expect something supernatural from God? If I could have rock hard abs by the end of writing this chapter, THAT would be awesome... and miraculous (and laughable according to my wife).

How do you define miracles? Without the help of Wikipedia, what would you say constitutes a honest-to-goodness miracle? Is a driveway oil spill in the shape of Jesus' face a miracle? That one really did make the news. There was also the tortilla in Mexico sporting Jesus' face. Someone built a shrine for that one. Spread the love, and pass the Miracle Whip. Unfortunately the Jesus tortilla was taken to grade school for show and tell, and it broke. The shrine and miracle came to an abrupt halt. My approach here is totally tongue-in-cheek, but I sincerely want to know: Were these things miracles? The miracle of the grilled cheese Jesus sandwich (which made serious money on Ebay), the fence with a Jesus shadow from nearby trees, the somewhat famous Jesus dental x-ray, the family in foreclosure with a huge maple tree Jesus knothole --- all of which claimed the miraculous by their respective discoverers.

Did God do this? How about the young couple with the miracle ultrasound? In their baby's ultrasound picture was the face of Jesus. That's enough to make a young expectant mother go, "Deja Mary!" Some who bend an elbow on St. Patrick's Day like the miracle of the legendary stein of beer. There in a frothy head of a Guinness was the face of Jesus. Was that really You, God? People everywhere are quite serious about these alleged, heavenly visitations. So many of these miracle sightings have been reported that one skeptical soul created a miracle parody of the phenomenon called the Jesus hickey. That one was not a miracle, but rather a really bad joke... and admittedly, I laughed out loud.

How do you define miracles, and do you have your theology together on this hot topic? If most of us want miracles (and I think we do), then what's our foundational thinking?

Most people think that the Bible is chock full of miracles. With every page turned, it seems, there is a great, big God doing one of His big, patented marvels. Actually, that kind of thinking is a bit far from the truth. There was a period in the Old Testament when God was forming a nation, and He did several miracles. Then there was a period when Jesus came on the scene in the New Testament, and He was establishing His Church. Jesus did several miracles then. Other than that, miracles are surprisingly sporadic throughout the Bible. In fact, if you were actually living in ancient Bible times, you would have thought miracles to be extremely rare, uncommon, and quite special. They just didn't happen all the time in people's driveways like many today think. There are actually many cases throughout the Bible where needed, wanted, and prayed for miracles simply did not occur.

The Apostle Paul was no stranger to supernatural wonders, but he also wrote how God's refusal of a miracle helped keep him from becoming conceited. God was pouring through Paul and his teaching, but allowed a "thorn" for Paul to contend with. Some scholars believe Paul had horrific eye troubles defining his thorn. Some are convinced he had problems with his legs, or that he was vertically challenged and did not like being short. Whatever it was, Paul asked God to miraculously take the physical disability away. Paul was convinced he could have served the Lord better if a miracle could remove the thorn. Instead, the thorn remained and Paul was kept humble. The thorn helped Paul to not sprout a spiritual fat head. God said no to Paul's request for a miracle. Jesus eventually responded and told Paul, *"My grace is sufficient for you, for my power is made perfect in weakness."* (II Corinthians 12:9) Oh shoot. Oh, God. No miracle.

Epaphroditus is a little-known name found in the New Testament. Apparently he got very sick. He almost died. He was a faithful worker and lover of God. He almost keeled over being an ambassador for Jesus. Don't you think at some point the people around Epap would have prayed for a miracle? A logical and powerful prayer would have asked God to whip out one of His big healing miracles for poor Epap. Not only did God not provide Epaphroditus a miracle, the poor guy almost died. And so we have another example of a non-miracle in the Bible (Philippians 2:25-30).

Why even bring this up and bring you down? It's because most Christians practically believe walking with Jesus should produce miracles 24/7, left and right, and in mostly big shapes and sizes. In reality, miracles in the Bible are rare and often times didn't happen even when asked for. The same is true today. The good news is that if miracles aren't happening all the time in your life, it doesn't mean God has forgotten you. You haven't slipped off His radar screen. Perhaps your non-miracle is God's way of getting your attention. God might be saying, "Listen, I want you to stop trusting in what I do for you, and start trusting in Me."

With a more balanced approach towards miracles, let's look at a couple of Jesus' miracles, and see if we can find application that makes sense --- or as much sense as the miraculous can make. Let's start with the words of Jesus. Are they miraculous?

Jesus went into a town called Capernaum, which was nestled next to the Sea of Galilee. Capernaum was several hundred feet below sea level, and was in large part a place of wet, marshy, lowlands. Malaria outbreaks in the ancient world were well-known there. Many people died from this mosquito-carried plague. Malaria always has a very high fever attached to its sting. Unfortunately I know about Malaria. Having been diagnosed with this exact same disease from a mission trip to Kenya, I know all about the fever and horrors of malaria. 105 to 106 degree fevers are common when malaria invades the body.

Jesus was teaching in the malaria epicenter of Capernaum. The people were literally blown away by His words. When was the last time you were blown away by the words of Jesus? Jesus' message carried an authoritative punch. His words even scared the demons possessing the fever-fried minds of malaria victims.

At the beginning of the Bible, Satan is told he will be crushed underneath the heels of Jesus. You wonder if in Capernaum, demons are fearful this is the beginning of the crushing end. Nobody has been able to touch them, but now these demons are wondering if Jesus will destroy them. Jesus tells the demons to be quiet, but the Greek words Jesus uses indicates a muzzling of an animal. "You are all animals. Shut up. Be muzzled. You have no power!" Suddenly and decidedly a demon leaves a man. Make no rookie mistake. This is a definitive miracle. That's the way Bible miracles go. Nobody was scratching their head saying, "Would you place that one under a miracle heading? I just couldn't tell without the Spielberg special effects." Like a pink yes on a first-time mom's pregnancy test, you would have spotted this decisive miracle in a Hebrew heartbeat.

In the first century, weird cults and religions tried to exorcise demons. People attempted this a lot. They would gather ginger or dandelion root and stuff it up people's noses to force the exit of demons. Don't try this at home. The whole ordeal was painful, slow, and usually didn't work too well. When Jesus removed a demon, He did so decidedly. People would have been absolutely wide-eyed as they scored a huge point on the miracle scoreboard for Jesus.

After Jesus amazes and astounds with said miracle, the Bible says people were blown away at His teaching. His what? Yep, His teaching. His words. Sometimes when you read the Bible, it's helpful to ask yourself what wasn't said. At Capernaum, what isn't said is, "That was a smokin' miracle!" Instead they talk about Jesus' words. They surmise it was His words forcing demons to flee, and not some kind of weird dandelion technique. News and excitement about Rabbi Jesus's words begin to spread as fast as a stolen kidney urban legend on the Internet.

In Jesus's day, there was a glut of rabbis who were really boring. Jewish teachers and leaders would give tired sermons able to put a Mountain Dew injected teenager into a religious coma. Rabbis waxed boorishly long because they learned boxy tradition, Old Testament law, and Torah from older, crotchety rabbis. Whatever they learned from older rabbis was simply passed down through lifeless teaching. It was all very tedious and dreary, but deemed necessary because, "That's the way we've always done it." Some things never change, especially in church world.

Occasionally a rogue rabbi would stroll into town. They would flaunt their own interpretations. These were independent, free thinkers. They were able to draw huge crowds. Their own personal stories and applications set them apart from rabbis who got stuck in merely repeating what had been repeated for years upon insipidly long years. Rabbis who would speak for themselves and spoke with authority would say things like, "You have heard it said, but I tell you..." Rabbis with such command and chutzpah were said to have *schmika*. Ancient Jewish people loved rabbis with schmika and would travel by foot for miles to hear the words of a teacher with this kind of power and authority.

When was the last time Jesus's words blew you away? When was the last time His miraculous words of salvation rocked your world? When was the last time His words of authority put life back into your, dusty, rusty, crusty, old, predictable label of *Christian*?

Words are powerful. A brief look at politics makes my point. At a media-hyped Iowa caucus, a Republican candidate beat out the front-runner who had a more lucrative bank account. The cable news channels were buzzing. Most pundits believed Mike Huckabee won the primary because he refused to use negative words. Television anchors were saying the entire political landscape of America had been changed with this unique approach. Wow. Really? All because of words. Huckabee refused to run negative ads, and won the war with well-chosen words.

An elder at our church, a person who I count as one of our most deep and overtly spiritual thinkers, sent me an email. He had a question. "Alan, think about this. If corn oil comes from corn, and vegetable oil comes from vegetables, where does baby oil come from?" That's just sick, but words can also make us laugh, can't they? Words challenge us. Words make us think. Words change our perceptions of elders.

Occasionally, I bring an unsuspecting person to the stage on a Sunday morning and place them in what I call *the affirmation seat*. Usually I try to find someone in need of a little encouragement. Once my subject is seated, I ask the rest of the Church to shout words of encouragement to the thirsty soul. Invariably I will hear people scream words like, "You're the greatest. You're awesome! We love you. You're a child of the most-high God. Jesus loves you. You rock. You're a child of God. You're a great mom." Even the sound guy gets in on the action and blurts, "Karen, you are fearfully and wonderfully made!" (I like a sound man who can bust out a little scripture at the drop of a microphone.) How do you think these words of affirmation felt to Karen? To a person like Karen, who had strung together a couple of rough years, I'm sure it felt pretty good.

We know the power of words. Why then do we so often ask for spectacular, sensational, miraculous stuff, and neglect the powerfully miraculous words of Christ? Jesus said mind boggling things like, "I am the way and the truth and the life. No one comes to the Father except through me." (John 14:6) Whoa. Those are incredible words. Why would someone hear those words of eternal rescue and say, "Yeah, but give me something REALLY cool."

Henry Blackaby writes, "If Jesus could speak and raise the dead, calm a storm, cast out demons, and heal the incurable, then what effect might a word from Him have upon your life?"[1] How miraculous are the very words of Christ? Do you approach the Word(s) of God with a holy expectation of the miraculous?

Jesus leaves the synagogue and goes to the home of Simon. It seems Simon's mother-in-law is suffering from a high fever. We would guess, being in Capernaum or its marshy suburbs, that malaria is the likely culprit. This is life-threatening. Malaria requires more than a few ibuprofen to bring the temperature down. With the thermometer rising to 105 or 106, this is one sick puppy of a mother-in-law. People in such dire straits, more often than not, died in ancient Capernaum. Sadly, malaria still ravages third world countries today. Jesus rebukes, chastises, and wags a dissenting finger at the malaria bug. The fever breaks immediately. Then Jesus just starts showing off. The woman jumps out of bed and begins waiting on Jesus and the other guests. Isn't that cool? It isn't as if Jesus told her to be healed, and then she stays in bed to finish her ten-day supply of antibiotics. Miracles in the Bible are without a doubt, and unambiguously so.

To keep our balanced perspective, I'm reminded how even authentic miracles of healing still have a 100 percent mortality rate. Sorry for that wet blanket, but let's keep digging.

When the sun was setting on a Saturday, religious ceremony was officially over and business as usual resumed for the ancient, middle-eastern Jew.

With the Sabbath ending, people were allowed to bring people to see Jesus. Sick people, possessed people, blind and lame people all came for a miraculous healing. Jesus physically touched and loved people one at a time. You didn't see too many boring, stuffy, old rabbis doing that kind of thing. I hope you can see how incredibly cool this was for Jesus to operate beyond the normal rabbinical M.O. After all, Rabbi Jesus had Schmika! Immediate and miraculous healings were followed by more demons silenced and hurled back into the smoky pits of hell where they belonged. Jesus spoke and unbelievable things happened. This was heady stuff. This was the stuff of miracles from the mouth and words of Jesus.

Where does your opinion land concerning the stuff of miracles? Some people are resolved that the miracles within the Bible never happened. Some think there are no additional miracles, and never will be. If you find yourself standing somewhere within those hard lines, you have to awkwardly deal with the resurrection. If you are a miracle skeptic, what will you do with the resurrection? THAT was a miracle.

Jesus died a horrific and violent death. Three short Jewish days later He was alive. It was a resurrection miracle. Only eight other individuals through the thousands of years covered by God's Word experienced this rarity. (There was a time when several people came back to life when Jesus was killed, but that was a total group thing.) Once Jesus burst forth from His cave tomb, He appeared to over 500 people at different times. This would have validated a physical, real, holy cow, resurrection miracle.

Some write this particular miracle off and claim Jesus really didn't die. He was beat up real good. He suffered severely and came close to death, but He recovered. He never actually died. It's amazing what those electrolytes in Gatorade can do! There's yet another ancient rumor about Jesus' body being stolen. Desperate disciples would have done anything to keep their cause and uprising alive, right? Wrong. Would you die for a lie? Almost every Apostle did die for the mission of Jesus. They died believing Jesus is alive, and many were sent to their own funerals through violent means. So much for the bogus stolen body theory.

Millions of people have given their very lives for the resurrected Jesus. If you don't believe in miracles, what on earth do you do with this divine resurrection miracle and the testimonies that would fill up every NFL stadium several times over? If you write off miracles, you have to wrestle with Jesus either being a liar or a lunatic, because as Lord He totally resurrected. [2] That's what you're up against when you're set against the ideas of miracles.

Some people will bridge the miracle gap claiming miracles did occur but have since stopped. This flavor of miracle doubter is called a cessationist. Put that on your business card. I Corinthians 13 becomes the banner text for a cessationist. When, as the Bible says, we were children, and we acted like a children, but then the perfect came. The perfect, some believe, is the Church and the completed Word of

God. There was a time, some believe, when miracles were like a scaffolding. They're no longer needed since the Church and the entirety of the Bible is established.

What do you believe in your theological gut about miracles? Did you use the free white space to write down a needed miracle, but are unsure of what you actually believe about that miracle happening? In other words, if your mouth would articulate, "God, I need a miracle," would your theology permit it to happen?

My Grandma Scott was a grand, old, Pentecostal, charismatic, Godly woman whom I loved spending long weekends with during the summer. The summer I turned nine years old, I headed off to Grandma's. I grew up in a different flavor of church from my Grandma. At my church we didn't talk much about the Holy Spirit. We seldom clapped, and our theology was neatly figured out. When I went to my grandmother's house that summer of 1969, I took my hay fever, allergies, and theology with me. All three were a bit of a mess.

After sneezing and blowing and coughing, Grandma got tired of my miserable routine. She hauled me off to her Thursday night healing church service. I remember this quite vividly. We went down into a packed, dark basement of someone's house. We resolutely took our seats in a row of cold, metal, folding chairs. Only the shouting of a man down front masked the damp, musty smell of the basement. There was a yelling preacher hitting people on the head and causing them to lay out flat on the sweaty cement floor. This was not my mother's church. It was, however, Grandma's. Without warning, my beloved grandmother (God bless her miracle-believing soul) grabbed my hand, and dragged me up the makeshift aisle to the front of the very dangerous space where the very loud preacher dude was. I had never seen this kind of stuff before from the back of any church, much less from the front row. The loud pastor said a few words and tapped me on the head. Nothing. There was charismatic bedlam and all kinds of spiritual activity going on all around me. Nothing was actually happening with me. Well, except for the fact that I stopped sneezing. That was cool. Grandma took me back to our metal chairs, and within 10 seconds my annoying sneeze pierced the Spirit-filled air again. Grandma gave me one of those looks that said, "I really can't wait for your father to pick you up."

What's my theology and thinking on miracles? Where do I land? I'm prone, these days, to approach God with humility. I want Jesus to determine the size and shape of miracles in my life. I hope for the miraculous backed by purpose. I certainly don't have all this figured out. I hope I never will, but that's where I'm currently landing. I do think praying about the mission and purpose behind miracles is a very good thing to do. If there isn't purpose behind miracles, can't things get weirdly skewed like the goofy stuff so prevalent on Christian TV?

As Jesus was wrapping things up at Capernaum, the people were trying to keep Him from leaving. I love that. I love the realness of the Bible. If Jesus had just completely healed your city's sick, lame, deaf, and blind, would you want Him to hitch hike to the next town? No way! You wouldn't want Him to go anywhere but your dining room where He could chill and take miraculous care of your every need.

It's interesting how earlier in Dr. Luke's fourth chapter there are people who want Jesus dead because of His words. His words of authority are convicting, challenging, and embarrassing. Because of His teaching and schmika, people want Him dead. But in Capernaum, people want Jesus to hang out and hang a shingle. Those are two fairly broad spectrums of what people want to do with Jesus.

What do you want to do with Him? Are you tired and done with His teaching? Do Jesus' words convict, irritate, or bore you to the point you want Him gone? If this is you, do you still want a miracle… or two?

Jesus tells His adoring fans in Capernaum He MUST leave because He has to… preach. THAT is very interesting. He doesn't say He has to hit the road because He wants to do more miracles somewhere else. He has to preach more good news to more people. Jesus is taking us to school on the real purpose and mission of miracles.

Jesus identifies preaching as the reason He was sent. It is why He exorcised the demon. It is why the malaria melted off the mother-in-law. Jesus tells His religious admirers the reason He does all the cool stuff they like is because of the message. Miracles helped substantiate the message. It's about lost people saved and restored. It's about the gospel… the good news of God coming to earth to be with us. Jesus doesn't have a driving need for the spectacular, but He does have a passion for broken people. This is the rocket fuel for the miraculous.

Jesus knows the sensational tends to distract from the mission. Miracles, as Jesus understands, don't necessarily change somebody's heart. Did a friend just pop into your head, that if God would just deliver a whopper, they would believe? "Jesus, a miracle or two would bring them to you!" Have you ever prayed that? I have.

Take a quick glance at the period in the Old Testament when miracles were happening left and right. God was establishing His people and nation of Israel. He was parting the Red Sea, raining bread from heaven, providing miracle quail for food, physically guiding His people with clouds and fire, and using rocks as water faucets. Those seemingly fortunate people back in the good 'ole days of the Old Testament had it made, didn't' they? Nope. Packaged in with all those spectacular miracles were a difficult lot of people. They seldom obeyed and often longed for the comfort and nostalgia afforded by the shackles of slavery. How's that for rational thinking? They wanted to go back to Egypt and captivity. They wanted to exchange Jehovah for a smaller "g" god, even in the middle of a miracle frenzy.

Doesn't this tell us something about miracles Jesus clearly knows? Miracles alone don't necessarily change hearts. This is a sad, human fact. Jesus made sure every one of His miracles had purpose and mission behind it. Miracles played an important role in Jesus's ministry, but His priorities were on prayer and preaching. Jesus had a mission for the lost. Everything Jesus did (including his cool miracles) was all about salvation. It's so easy for us to forget this.

How do we get so sidetracked that salvation is just a ho-hum God thing? How do we lose sight of the modern day miracle of Jesus resurrecting Himself within anyone who chooses to die to self? It's why I absolutely love and celebrate baptisms as freshly redeemed souls go home wet. Salvation should blow us away. We should still be amazed at the schmika and authority coming through the words of Jesus that save us.

I can remember Becky and Perry. They were a messy couple baptized on a cold December Sunday morning. They had a bad history of drugs, arrests, kids taken away by the State, and a relationship of convenience outside of God's design for marriage. Becky and Perry were far from the westernized idea of being a Christian.

The miracle of salvation swept them off their feet when they were completely powerless to do anything for themselves. On the same Sunday the Bishops were baptized, several gracious ladies of our church creatively put together a small wedding ceremony and reception. It was a grand day in the Kingdom. It was a salvation party Jesus DID attend. We were all front row ticket holders to the miracle of salvation. Although Becky and Perry still don't live perfect lives, they have received and hung onto their perfect miracle. The undeniable miracle of salvation is something real Christians and authentic churches should elevate and pray for.

Henry Blackaby writes, "The difference between a church and a social club is the miraculous."[3] The miraculous should be a part of the Christian experience. We either believe nothing is impossible with God or everything is. Personally, I never want to box God into a no-miracle zone ever again. Let God be God because He can do whatever He wants. What about that face of Jesus on a grilled cheese sandwich? Maybe that IS a miracle after all. Maybe.

Here's what I am totally sure of: A lost person who is far from God can gain eternal security. That is a spectacular thing only a supernatural and miraculous God can do. That is a miracle by anyone's definition. Which do you think is the greater miracle? Is it forgiveness, and somebody far from God connecting? Is it a cured disease? Many believers who need to prop up their weak label of *Christian* will struggle with this if they are brutally honest. Salvation is OK, but a stage-4 cancer healing would really boost our religious ratings. Remember: A healed disease still has a 100 percent mortality rate, and not everybody is changed by a miracle. However, a soul changed and saved for all eternity by the blood and resurrection of Jesus is the quality of miracle no Hollywood script or cheesy TV preacher can duplicate.

I'm convinced, now more than when Grandma Scott was around, real Christians should pray for miracles. We should pray for God's hand to do things we're not used to. Jesus followers should expect to be surprised. With humility and a predetermination on how God will decide the size and shape of miracles, we should boldly ask for them. We should ask for purpose to be attached. If you need a financial miracle, pray your brains out. Ask for a lost person to somehow be attached to your prayer. If a marriage miracle is needed, pray and attach mission to that miracle. If you're praying for a relational miracle, try tacking on purpose, vision, and mission. That's the way Jesus did it. When the miracle maze gets confusing, always go back to the way Jesus did it. Always.

We need a miracle, don't you think? Christians need a miracle. Christians need a few authentic miracles from an authentic God to authenticate our faith and reverse our current PR problem as card carrying Christians. Following Jesus is a miraculous pursuit. Wearing the title of *Christian* has become everything but. What if we gave up the quest for the spectacular and simply followed Jesus? What if Jesus had permission to do what He needs to do to accomplish His purpose, passion, vision, and mission in our lives? That would be a miracle. We need a miracle.

Did you actually use the suggested white space at the beginning of this chapter? Did you write down a miracle you need? Now try affixing God's purpose, Christ's mission, and your humility to your request. Ask away! You would be setting aside self. Your request would be a blow to stuffy, consumer religion. You would be following Jesus AND regaining lost ownership of our cherished label. How's that for a miracle?

Chapter End Notes

1. Henry Blackaby, <u>Experiencing God Day By Day</u>, Jan. 4
2. Lewis, C.S., <u>Mere Christianity</u>, London: Collins, 1952, p54-56.
3. Henry Blackaby, <u>Experiencing God Day By Day</u>, Dec. 26.

Chapter Five

Click, Reply, Delete

Strategy #5: Stop trying to be the expert.

Luke 5:1-11

"One day as Jesus was standing by the Lake of Gennesaret, with the people crowding around him and listening to the word of God, he saw at the water's edge two boats, left there by the fishermen, who were washing their nets. He got into one of the boats, the one belonging to Simon, and asked him to put out a little from shore. Then he sat down and taught the people from the boat. When he had finished speaking, he said to Simon, "Put out into deep water, and let down the nets for a catch." Simon answered, "Master, we've worked hard all night and haven't caught anything. But because you say so, I will let down the nets." When they had done so, they caught such a large number of fish that their nets began to break. So they signaled their partners in the other boat to come and help them, and they came and filled both boats so full that they began to sink. When Simon Peter saw this, he fell at Jesus' knees and said, "Go away from me, Lord; I am a sinful man!" For he and all his companions were astonished at the catch of fish they had taken, and so were James and John, the sons of Zebedee, Simon's partners. Then Jesus said to Simon, "Don't be afraid; from now on you will catch men." So they pulled their boats up on shore, left everything and followed him."

How do you decide what e-mails you're going to open? Which ones will you quickly delete? I receive hundreds of e-mails a week. The volume of dreaded forwards has trained me to perform quick electronic triage to determine life or death to the flood of my inbox. Good portions of these ridiculous messages are strange religious ones. They're always flagged as something every Christian must read. Sometimes the subject line will brag, "The most beautiful thing you will ever see." Once you open it, you realize it's the most stupid thing you wish you'd never seen. At the end of utter lameness, such e-mails command the reader to pass it along to ten friends. If you don't, you'll break a magical prayer chain. If you don't, you go straight to hell. Seriously? I'm beyond tired of such strange cyberspace religion.

There is a rebellious resolve within me to never feel guilty when I delete those stupid notes. I always break the chain. I'm the guy. I do it with great joy. Please don't send me those weird e-mails unless you want ten other people to have unanswered prayers and go straight to hell too. It's a very easy decision for me to click, delete, and move on.

The Bible has many stories of people who show great faith, and others who get stuck on weak religion. Marginalized, hurting people within scripture often display an active faith towards Jesus, while high-church folks turn away. Every one of these people makes similar decisions with Jesus that we make with our e-mail. Should I click, reply, send, or just delete?

What are you going to do with Jesus? Everybody, at some point in his or her life, will have a real encounter with the living Jesus. You will have to make some sort of decision. Will the Creator become your personal default page, or just another file in your trash bin? What will you do with Jesus?

Here's a deeper question. What will it take for us to be Jesus followers beyond the bubble of what Christian marketers have placed us in? I'm convinced the totality of our Christianity is not merely having all of the right words memorized. Jesus wants more than our Sunday morning behavior perfected. It can't be just about creating lists of what secular things not to do during the week. Stuffing your days full of "Christian only" stuff just cannot be the point. If following Jesus is my only goal, what will that look like? Will it be messy? Will I look and feel more like a slick, professional Christian? Sometimes my pursuit of being a Christian gets in the way of actually serving and following Jesus. When that happens, I know something is off track.

In Luke chapter five, Jesus is found standing on the shore of Lake Gennesaret. Gennesaret is a rather large body of water. It's also called the Sea of Galilee. The water is some 700 feet below sea level, and the surrounding mountains tower some 2,000 feet above. To gain a mental snapshot, think of a large cereal bowl minus the milk and Cap'n Crunch. With its precarious setting, violent storms can quickly swell on a warm day. Hundreds of fishermen make their living on Lake Gennesaret. These are skilled, hard-working, meticulous fishermen who know how to navigate and weather sudden storms.

A sardine packing company is part of the Biblical landscape attached to Lake Gennesaret. Sardines are plentiful and make for a profitable, smelly export. Fishing for sardines is hard work requiring two boats with strong nets to catch the tiny fish.

Jesus sees two boats on the water's edge left by fishermen who are cleaning and washing their nets. The mates who own these boats are recognized professionals. They are experts. Jesus is encountering some of the most serious, commercial anglers this part of the world has seen. These are not your average weekend warriors dropping a thin line and plastic bobber into the water.

After getting into one of the vacated boats, Jesus wants to go for a lake cruise. Once on the lake, Jesus and Simon position themselves a short distance from shore. From this vantage point, Jesus begins teaching to people on shore. There is a crowd of people hanging on Jesus's every word. The hardcore fishermen who, seem to be off to one side of the story, are showing little interest. The fishermen are noticeably not where everyone else is. Fishing nets needed some attention, so they were absorbing this Jesus encounter from a distance.

Is Simon (also tagged as Peter) one who is intrigued but not convinced? He is in the boat. He's closer. Is Peter all in or simply checking Jesus out at with a bit more proximity? The Bible writer Matthew tells how Peter accepted the call to follow Rabbi Jesus. In a Biblical blur, Peter and his brother, Andrew, dropped their nets and signed up for a three-year tour with Jesus. Matthew says, "At once, they left their nets and followed Him." (Matthew 4:20)

The occasion of Peter following Jesus at once, and Jesus teaching from a vacated boat, are two different stories. In Dr. Luke's story, Peter is still checking Jesus out. This has just as much to say about Jesus as it does Peter. Jesus will go as fast or slow as we want, but He will never force anyone to follow. He will always give you space. Fishermen in Dr. Luke's story are not fully committed... yet. This is a great vignette of Jesus's patience as people process the idea of becoming serious, radical followers.

Jesus was a trained carpenter. When he finishes this lakeside teaching session, He says something very presumptuous to Peter. Jesus tells the fishing expert to paddle into deeper water and throw out the nets. Isn't it ironic how a carpenter is telling a fisherman what to do? Simon Peter responds with a grumbling, "Master..." This is not some quasi-religious garb Peter is flinging out. He is not labeling Jesus as the Messiah or anything divinely special. Peter is accentuating that Jesus is a teacher and not a fisherman. This would also highlight Peter's pride in his obvious smelly occupation. The word "master" in the original Greek language can also mean "supervisor." Can you sense the tension in their boat? Peter must be thinking, "Jesus, you're a carpenter and a teacher. You want to supervise me in catching sardines? THAT is a hoot, AND a bit frustrating. What in the world do YOU know about fishing?" It's almost laughable how Peter begins questioning the

Creator who made the fish, until we realize how often we do exactly the same.

I easily forget how the Creator who designed sardines knows best how to catch them. My expertise tends to cloud the waters. When I gather my most logical senses, I know I'm outmatched to question God in any circumstance. Remarkably, I still can doubt the Creator's supervision of my life.

With a sarcastic sigh, Peter informs his untrained supervisor how he had worked all night (the absolute best time to catch fish), and now the pickings were slim. I love this next part. Peter lets out a very teenage-esque, " But because YOU say so, I'll do it." By the way, some people believe Peter could have actually been a teenage fisher dude. Do you hear his slanted attitude towards Jesus? I can hear it because I have teenagers who offer the same tone, words, and approach. "Dad, it's not going to rain. But because YOU say so, I'll take an umbrella."

The dynamics unfolding in our story are fishy, but fun to digest. A traveling, former-carpenter, itinerant Rabbi tells an expert fisherman to throw out one net. He wants Peter to fish from one boat and in broad daylight. You can't do that! It takes two boats, several nets, and sardines are caught at night. Everyone knows that! Being behind on the monthly quota of sardines makes this whole scene even more exasperating for a bewildered fisherman like Peter.

When the fishing advice of a carpenter is reluctantly taken, there is a catch of sardines one net can't hold. Other expert fishermen are called to bring their boats to help. These are the other fishermen who earlier stood at a distance listening to Jesus teach. They hurriedly splash their way out to the deeper waters where Jesus and Peter are having the catch of a lifetime. The extra boats begin to sink because the nets are so heavily packed like… uh, sardines. More irony. As the boats begin to sink, an up-close look at the Messiah is given to the previously distanced fishermen. I try to imagine how wide-eyed these guys are as their heads move back and forth from the fish to Jesus and back to the fish.

Is it possible Jesus wants to use our expertise, but in His way and not necessarily ours? Isn't it possible that our expertise can get in the way of serving Jesus if we believe we can fish better than the God who created the fish?

For me, the older I get, the smarter I become. The longer I walk with Jesus, the better I think I know how the kingdom works. That's exactly when Jesus says, "No, Alan, I appreciate your expertise and the talents you've developed. I DO want to use your expertise, but I want to use it MY way."

God whispers to us, "My thoughts are not your thoughts [although you think you're an expert]." God reminds each of us, "My ways higher than your ways and My thoughts than your thoughts." (Isaiah 55:8-9)

Isn't it interesting how Dr. Luke jumps from writing Simon to Simon Peter? This is the same guy, but with two different names. What's the difference between the two? Peter is synonymous with "rock." You may have heard about this. This fisherman moonlights as a WWF wrestler on the weekends. He is Simon the Rock. Simon the Rock falls to his knees.

Like Hulk Hogan kneeling to his ex, Simon the Rock grasps the knees of Jesus and calls Him Lord.

What does he call Jesus? Lord. Previously Jesus was a teacher… a supervisor… a carpenter out of his element… a teacher who couldn't bait a hook. "Lord" means Almighty, sovereign God, and the Messiah. "Lord" is a deeper, significant word.

Peter doesn't view himself as the expert any longer. Something has shifted. Instead, Peter's self-image has been re-framed as a sinner. The presumptuous comparisons have stopped. Jesus is holy, perfect, and the Almighty. Making a comparison to the perfection and majesty of God is never a good one to make. You wake up and realize who you really are. You're broken. You are not worthy of such a comparison, and you begin doing Isaiah's holy monologue.

The Old Testament prophet, Isaiah, is given a grand vision of the Lord seated on a throne. His glory is compared to His robe filling the temple. Non-computer-generated creatures are flying circles overhead saying, "Perfect, perfect, perfect. Holy, holy, holy is the Lord." The glory, weight, significance and Hebrew *kavod* of God is thick. Isaiah gets a supernatural glimpse of God and immediately declares his ruin. With holy fear Isaiah knows the reality of his imperfection. He is a sinner who can't stand in the presence of God.[1]

When you and I have such an encounter with God, we too are toast. Burnt toast is useless. When we arrive at such a point God smiles. Why would He do that? That smile signals He can finally use us.

Knowing who we are because we remember who He is, allows God to be the Supervisor in any and every situation.

Peter, the Rock, is astonished at the catch of fish. Those other aloof fishermen are blown away too. This includes James and John whom folks call "The Sons of Thunder." They were more egotistical WWF wrestlers. Jesus tells the expert, seasoned, skilled fishermen, "Don't be afraid." I love the savvy confidence of Jesus. I love how Jesus never wastes a word or experience. After the sardine catch of the first century, Jesus addresses their fear. What was their fear? They are fishermen who just took in the mother load. What are they afraid of?

Jesus is all about fish. Although you can make a fairly good argument that Jesus can't bait a hook, Jesus is all about fish. Jesus talks about fish. He alludes to fish in His teaching. He metaphorically refers to fish. In fact, Jesus so identifies Himself to and with fish that early Christians used a fish symbol to identify themselves. The Greek word for fish is *ichthus*. Ichthus became a sort-of acronym for "Jesus Christ, God's Son and Savior." In ancient times, underground Christians scratched fish symbols on walls and street corners to identify gathering spots. Some of you may have an ichthus on the back of your car. Literally this means you're having a church service in your mini van! (Maybe those French fries on the floor could be communion bread.) An ichthus is a powerful symbol tying you to the passion and mission of Jesus.

Jesus is all about lost people being saved. Fishing. He's all about making disciples who follow and imitate Him. Shouldn't we be about the same thing, especially if we have one of those plastic fish plastered to the back of our Chevys? Shouldn't we be all about lost people? But do we have to give up everything to fish? Jesus' expert fishing friends did. Was that what they were afraid of?

Jesus challenges these surprised fishing buddies, and the Bible says, "They pulled their boats up on shore, left everything, and followed Him." Great. This means that you and I need to quit our jobs. We should move to primitive jungles where the real heathen fish are. Is this right? Nope.

Factoring in the Holy Spirit becomes a very necessary component to our sardine miracle story. During Jesus's days on earth, you needed to be physically in the presence of Jesus (or close proximity) to be influenced by Him. You had to hang out with Him.

Certain people decided they really wanted to be influenced by Rabbi Jesus. Such people DID give up their jobs, their livelihoods, and determined to physically be with Jesus. There was a difference in how the Holy Spirit operated then compared with today. The Holy Spirit had not been fully poured out when Jesus was giving fishing lessons by the lake. Jesus also promised He would send the Holy Spirit some day to replace His physical presence. Jesus mysteriously said when the Holy Spirit came; we would do even greater things than He did (John 14:12). The Holy Spirit would facilitate the presence of Jesus in each of us without having to actually be with Jesus. Cool, huh? Now we can have the presence of Jesus wherever we are. Wherever we are, we can have the power of the Holy Spirit. You don't have to leave everything to be in the physical presence of Jesus.

Don't be afraid. You don't have to give up your jobs to fish or be influenced by Jesus. You don't have to sell the family sardine business in order to be a fisherman for Jesus. In fact, I have seen very effective executives bring a lot of people to Jesus. I have seen real estate agents be very effective fishermen in the Kingdom. I have seen lawyers, in spite of all the lawyers in hell jokes, be very effective fishers of men. On the other hand, I've watched other effective Kingdom people declare their arrival and insist God wants them to give it all up and reach the pinnacle of ministry by becoming full-time pastors. Many of those effective people lose their effectiveness by becoming a full-time pastor. They give up Jesus to become a professional Christian. That is a ding dang Kingdom shame.

A full-time pastor is not the epitome of effectiveness in the Kingdom. Trust me. I know all about that. Jesus tells Simon the Rockmeister, "Don't be afraid." Why? Why would a bunch of fishermen be afraid of a bunch of fish? Is it because their boats almost sank? Remember, Simon and the others are intrigued by Jesus, but only from a distance. The chasm between Jesus and these professional anglers is filled by the security of their jobs. Their hope, confidence, and trust are tied up in those tangled nets.

This is how they make money and take care of their families. They have a strong confidence in self.

Jesus is extremely patient in their emerging followership. He waits and loves them even if they insist on observing from the sidelines. It is becoming time, however, to jump into the sea without a net. Jesus's puzzling words, "don't be afraid," point to everything that makes them secure and confident. This one is tough to argue. Jesus just out-fished the pros by 1,000 to one. He took them to school, and then asked if they would put their trust in the real expert.

You may or may not be called out of your job and into full-time ministry. However, everyone one of us will be challenged by Rabbi Jesus to change our priorities. Jesus looks each of us squarely between the eyes of our purses and wallets and says, "Will you stop trusting yourself, and follow Me instead?"

A friend of mine did this very thing. Putting trust and security into the hands of God is a big deal for a talented man like Kuk. If you're familiar with the song "Umbrella" by Rihanna, then you know Kuk. He helped write and produce that monster hit. Kuk won a Grammy for his excellent work on "Umbrella" and has won several more for his collaboration with artists like Mary J. Blige, Beyonce, and Justin Bieber. In all the hype and glam, Kuk is very aware of the God factor. In fact, sometimes on Sunday mornings, you can see Kuk in the children's ministry leading worship and helping the knee nippers. He does this to stay grounded in his faith.

Kuk will openly give praise to God for 100 percent of his whirlwind life and says it's all a God deal. Initially, God found my friend in a hard place of being absolutely broke and spiritually lost. In 1992, Kuk and his wife Stevie were saved. God proceeded to pull Kuk out of the record industry and into a full-time worship and kids' ministry.

Once God pulled Kuk into ministry, He taught the Harrells the value of worship. God taught Kuk why he was gifted --- to first and foremost worship Him. Kuk heard God say, "If I want you to go into the music industry, if I want you to be anywhere in the world, just let Me open up the doors for you. Let Me be the expert in using your expertise. When you go through those doors, you'll be assured you have every tool you'll need to stay with confidence and assurance, and know I have your back."

Sitting on top of the music world's heap, Kuk communicated back to God. "Okay, you know what, Lord? All of this is great, but it means absolutely nothing. Would You like for me to let this go tomorrow?" Kuk was OK if God took him away from the spotlight. If God told Kuk to give it all up and go back into full-time ministry, he would do it. He would do it because he knew wherever God called Kuk, God would give him everything he needed. Kuk's trust and security was in Jesus no matter the circumstance.

God has now blessed Kuk with a platform to speak and tell God's story. I saw him make a cameo appreance on American Idol the other night. Amazing. When you win a Grammy, most everyone in the music industry sees you as an expert. You are considered to be one of the best in what you're doing through music and production. People will listen. Kuk knows who the real Expert is.

Lately my world-traveling friend has been hearing God speak again. Kuk believes God indicated how too many other people have been getting credit for what God is doing in his life. It's time for Kuk to speak out. It's time for Kuk to let people know his success is all a God deal. The reality for my friend is that, like Jesus, becoming vocal about his faith may not go so well in the end. The possibility of rejection is very real for Kuk as he becomes a more visible, vocal, Jesus follower. Kuk is continuing to place his security, faith, and confidence in Jesus instead of his own expertise. God wants to use Kuk's expertise, but perhaps in His way.

Jesus's most common methodology is to use shepherds to lead people. He takes fishermen to catch lost people. He has a way of taking an executive to execute His grand plan. Jesus can use a nurse to come to someone's spiritual aid. With a surrendered heart, Jesus can use a salesman to pitch His plan of grace and restoration. Jesus can take a record producer and produce Kingdom results if we give it all up and over to Him. He's the real expert. Not us.

What will you do with Jesus, so you can see what He will do with you? Click. Reply. Delete?

There were once two boats so full of fish they almost capsized. This is normal fishing for Jesus. Normal fishing is not five skinny bluegills strung up on a string. Typical fishing, for Jesus, involves two boatloads full of lost people.

These days in China, thousands are coming to
t each week. In America, successful churches
00... maybe even 200... people coming to the
each year. This is considered a really good year.
t normal fishing for Jesus. What's the deal?
Maybe our expertise has gotten in the way.
e we've forgotten who we are, especially in light
Cross. Maybe we're not serious disciples who
o do what Jesus did. Maybe we've dropped our
nd turned the American Church into something
ng mere self-actualization. *"Bless me, feed me,
e worship, and if you don't, I'm just going to go
here else."* It all depends on where we're
our trust and confidence.

ather God, Your Word seems pretty clear.
pirit, as individuals and as Your Church, break
n. God, bring us to that holy point where we
"Woe is me! I'm not worthy. I'm a sinner. I'm
xpert in anything." God, bring those who
be Christians to the place where You can use
esus, we want to be all about fish. We want to
t what You are about. God, forgive us when
lfish. Forgive us when it is all about us. We
r trust, security, and lives into Your expert
Amen.

Chapter End Notes

ly Bible, New International Version; (Indianapolis, IN;
h 6:1-8.

Chapter Six

Play In The Dirt Again

Strategy #6: Believe eternal life is for now.

Luke 8:4-15

"While a large crowd was gathering and people were coming to Jesus from town after town, he told this parable: "A farmer went out to sow his seed. As he was scattering the seed, some fell along the path; it was trampled on, and the birds of the air ate it up. Some fell on rock, and when it came up, the plants withered because they had no moisture. Other seed fell among thorns, which grew up with it and choked the plants. Still other seed fell on good soil. It came up and yielded a crop, a hundred times more than was sown." When he said this, he called out, "He who has ears to hear, let him hear." His disciples asked him what this parable meant. He said, "The knowledge of the secrets of the kingdom of God has been given to you, but to others I speak in parables, so that, "
'though seeing, they may not see; though hearing, they may not understand.'

"This is the meaning of the parable: The seed is the word of God. Those along the path are the ones who hear, and then the devil comes and takes away the word from their hearts, so that they may not believe and be saved. Those on the rock are the ones who receive the word with joy when they hear it, but they have no root. They believe for a while, but in the time of testing they fall away. The seed that fell among

*thorns stands for those who hear, but as they go on
their way they are choked by life's worries, riches and
pleasures, and they do not mature. But the seed on
good soil stands for those with a noble and good
heart, who hear the word, retain it, and by persevering
produce a crop."*

This book should have come with a packet of
dirt. If it had, right about now is when I would have
you empty the contents into your hands, and hold it for
approximately two minutes. Don't just hold it; feel it.
Smell the dirt. Even now with only the imaginary soil
in your hands, can't you almost smell the smell of
dirt? It's the stuff every second-grade boy's recess is
made of. Meditate on the dirt. Be the dirt. No, not
really. That's just weird.

In the Old Testament book of Genesis, we find
the auspicious beginning and power of dirt. Genesis
2:7 is part of the creation account, and unfolds the
mystery of how God formed man from the dust, dirt,
and soil of the ground. God told mankind to be the
dirt. That's still a little weird. If you wanted to, you
could make a very convincing argument of how dirt is
attached to life. Dirt became so synonymous with life
that God determined we would all go back to it once
life is done.

It's interesting stuff, isn't it? Dirt. Next time
you wish you were weeding, planting, or harvesting,
but are stuck helplessly inside by the calamity called
winter, do a Bible study on dirt. See what you find.
See if your shovel unearths a passage like the ninth
chapter of John. Watch what happens when you
unearth some of this rich, New Testament soil.

In the first twelve verses of chapter nine, the Bible writer John portrays a guy who's been blind from birth. Some of Jesus' surrounding friends who are stuck in the grips of religion, presumptuously ask, "Why is this guy blind? Who sinned? Whose fault is it?" Sometimes religious people try to point out other's faults in order to keep the heat from exposing their own. Jesus deals succinctly with His religious friends, and then moves towards the man who couldn't see. I love this next part. It makes me want to play in the dirt again. Jesus removes His artistically painted halo, and spits on the ground. With a saliva-based paste, Jesus slaps the lifeless eyes of a sad blind man. Sphhllat! Once again we see how dirt and mud and soil are connected to life because this sightless man regains his with a miraculous healing from dirt.

Our pursuit of Jesus is a manhunt for eternal life. When we talk about life in the context of the Bible, eternal life is the big pay off. When you and I die we hope to go "up" to eternal life. When those evil people who make our lives miserable die, we hope they go "down" to their eternal life. We assume eternal life is for later. It's for somewhere down the line and in the future.

Jesus said eternal life is for now. Jesus puts a hurt on religion and explains how eternal life is knows God through Jesus, NOW (John 17:3). In case you missed it, this is one of those yellow highlighter moments in the New Testament. Religion tends to box up eternal life as something for later. Jesus points to an active, relational bond being the definition of eternal life now.

This idea of having eternal life now is exactly why William P. Young's classic, *The Shack* became an instant favorite of mine. It rocked a lot of theologian's worlds and destroyed many religious boxes. Young poignantly writes, "God is a verb." While that little phrase may not initially bowl you over, you should feel it and smell it like the imaginary dirt included with this book. There's life in that four-word offering.

God is a verb. He gives, loves, responds, sings, laughs, and dances. God is a verb, and as William P. Young says, "We turn Him into a noun."[1] We make God a place, an institution, a list of rules… a religion.

Many 16 to 29 year olds are incredibly open about opinions attached to church. This critical generation seems to scream, "Just give God to us straight, but don't give it if you're not living it." There's a label-weary generation wanting help to live out their faith now. Eternal life now. I want that too.

Why do you think we've turned God into a noun? Why is the Almighty consigned to a stale religion? That question is not as rhetorical as it may sound. I'm not sure we completely trust God anymore, and maybe some never did. Do we really believe God is good? In my most honest moments I know exactly whom I trust the most. It's me. I've asked God to prove His goodness, but often times I just can't see it the way I want to see it. That's when my God trust goes out the window. What should I do with such a God? I tend to control Him and put Him in a box.

One of the world's leading theologians, Sean Penn, once said, "When everything gets answered it's fake." Apply this insightful gem to our version of a boxed up belief system. We're not sure we can trust God. We're not convinced He's all that good, and so we wall Him in. We want black and white answers and neatly-wrapped theologies to be the packing tape on our God box. At some point we realize that with everything controlled, answered, and ticketed as *Christian,* all we have left is a lifeless, fake version of something we no longer want.

After following God and wearing the fading brand of Christian for over forty years, my reality has become simple. The more I try to follow the great I AM, the more questions I have. How does one really define the great I AM... alpha omega... who was, is, and is to come? Can we really put I AM in a corrugated box? Do you think God wants us to succinctly define Him? Have you heard about the whole golden calf incident and how mad God became? That was a rather famous Old Testament stunt to cram I AM into the constraints of cardboard... uh, gold...walls. It really ticked God off (Exodus 32:1-19). Don't you think God still gets a bit miffed when we stop seeing Him as a wonderfully active verb, and stuff Him into a boorishly controlled noun?

Life and relationship happens when we explore God as a verb. One of scripture's gems, The Parable of the Sower, tackles this very idea. It's a parable of dirt that most first-century folks could easily relate to. Our modern enlightenment must not keep us from playing in this same dirt again. Remember, there's life in the dirt.

In the first century, farming was quite different from today. Today's high tech farmers guide their big, green John Deere tractors to plow the ground before seeds can be planted. During Dr. Luke's day, everyone and their middle-eastern brother were farmers. It didn't take much. People would see a piece of land and throw out seed without plowing. After the planting, they would discover things like rocks, weeds, and old, abandoned roads within the dirt. Because of such haphazard planting techniques, seeds would have random destinations. Some would land on a path, some trampled on, and some snatched up by skinny birds. It was a percentage gamble ancient farmers willingly took. Some seeds fell on unfriendly rocks. Those rocky seeds might spring up, but would later wither without sustainable moisture and roots. You understand all of this, right? It's basic Farming 101.

Seeds were flung wildly in all directions like Tootsie Rolls hurled at parade kids. Ancient farmers would inadvertently land some kernels among a patch of thorns. The seeds would grow and get choked like a wild toddler sneaking said flung Tootsie Roll at aforementioned parade. Stay with me here. We've almost plowed our way through this parable. A good patch of dirt would also catch a few of the thrown seeds. This incredibly rich soil brought life and a bumper crop of a hundred fold. That's farmer talk for a lot. After Jesus gives a remedial lesson on farming,

He says something very curious. "He who has ears to hear let him hear." Was he talking corn here?

This is where we need to stop for a moment. Understand the application Jesus is trying to make. The earthy dynamics of farming are parallel tracking with eternal ramifications of Jesus' parable. Don't worry if you're a little lost. Even Jesus' best friends, who know well the antiquated farming methods, are standing around scratching their black-haired heads. They eventually break down and admit they didn't get it. To make things even worse, Jesus begins talking about secrets of the Kingdom of God.

Ever wonder why there are secrets in God's Kingdom, and why the Kingdom's King would use parables people might not understand? Why does it seem Jesus wants to make all of this hard to comprehend?

The Greek word for *secrets* can also point to the mystery surrounding the plans, purpose, and counsel of God. This is lofty stuff, which can take a lifetime to understand. Jesus can't be advocating a twisted game of hide-and-seek concerning the plans of God and the people He loves, can He? That would contradict scripture. What is going on here? Why are there so many secrets and mysteries?

Jesus was a Jewish rabbi who probably memorized the entire Old Testament. His teaching and recorded conversations are great proof of this. Jesus had a keen working knowledge of books like Isaiah. His early teen years would have been spent verbally sparring with older rabbis about the intricate workings of what we now call the fifth gospel. As an adult rabbi, Jesus would have been quick to recall Isaiah's dilemma of taking God's Word to people with poor listening skills and worse abilities to apply. It seems Isaiah's sixth chapter is ringing in the ears of Jesus as He talks to His friends about dirt. Sometimes God's Word is presented very clearly to people, but sometimes they just won't budge.

Take a glance at Isaiah 6:9. *"... Be ever hearing, but never understanding."* Go ahead and stare at the word *hearing.* In Hebrew the word is *shamah.* This Hebrew gem gives a picture of both hearing and obeying. Isaiah would preach. People would hear. There would still be a serious deficiency of obedience.

Meanwhile... back on the farm, Jesus is using dirt as a creative object lesson. Jesus is trying to explain how there will be people who hear His message, but they'll never obey. Jesus says, "He who has ears to hear let him hear." Rabbi Jesus seems to be expounding the ancient Hebrew/Jewish concept: hearing requires both listening and obeying. This being the case, why would the Messiah speak in confusing parables even close friends wouldn't understand? Why make this so complicated?

There's a rumor in Atlanta about Georgia Tech University. Seems they like to make life extremely difficult for incoming freshmen. My totally unreliable (and mostly UGA) sources tell me professors at GT like to really stick it to freshmen so they can weed out the bad apples. The only students they want forging ahead are the really hungry, top-notch, and future world-class engineers.

Why would Jesus purposefully make His teaching difficult?

Most parents have done this. Sometimes moms and dads have intentionally kept things vague with their kids. Great parenting techniques do allow for assigning tasks without giving detailed instructions. Why on earth would parents do that… for heaven's sake?

My wife turned a very sexy 41, and I went to my oldest daughters for some help with the celebration. I told my girls, "We could go to a restaurant, but I'm cheap. Let's do it all ourselves. Let's do a fancy dinner, and really do it up. I'll buy a great present and get the decorations, while you girls whip up a several-course meal and bake a great cake. OK?" I intentionally left out the details for my very capable girls. Predictably they began asking things like what to fix, how much, if the best china should be used, and how to get the groceries for the grand occasion. I told them, "Just figure it out!" Why would I purposefully leave them in a vague, black, birthday hole? Why would I allow them to swim in such a shallow pool of confusion? I do love them, don't I? I simply wanted them to approach this task as more than just a task. I wanted them to take deeper ownership of an indebted relationship with their wonderful mother.

Why does Jesus give permission for parables, mysteries, and secrets to be part of His Kingdom? Perhaps it's to determine how hungry we are. Maybe, like a GT graduate, it's to determine which of us really wants to wear the name *Christian* with all the rights, privileges, and responsibilities thereunto appertaining.

Maybe it's all about what we're hungry for and listening to. I heard a story recently of a Native American Indian who went to New York City for the very first time. He was with a close friend, and they were walking down a noisy New York street. Taxicabs were blowing their horns. Street vendors were shouting. Cashiers were ringing at hot dog stands. There was construction work, beeping cars, loud trucks, and rusty buses. In the middle of this urban symphony, the wide-eyed Indian turned to his friend and said, "I hear a cricket." Incredulously, the friend sputtered, "A what?" Without warning, the curious Indian was off to the races trying to find a single cricket. This crazy native went running down a city block, crossed the street, found a tree, and reached into a small knothole to pull out the chirping cricket. An amazed and winded friend said, "What was that all about? How did you do that?"

The satisfied Indian replied, "It's all in what you're listening for." His bewildered friend didn't get the point and expressed confusion. "I'm not sure I understand what you're saying." Moving into teacher mode, the Indian pulled out a pocket full of change, and lifted it high into the air. "Watch this!" The fist full of coins went flying and clanging onto the hard concrete. Fifty city folk immediately turned to see what was unfolding. With professor-like confidence, the Indian concluded, " It's all in what you're listening for. It's all in what you're hungry for."[2]

What are you hungry for? What perks your ears up these days? What kind of dirt is in your hands?

What kind of life are you holding on to? Anyone need to play in the dirt again?

Even with a quest to see how hungry spiritual seekers are, Jesus gives the meaning of His dirt parable. Jesus finally gives a straightforward response to His friends and says, "OK, here's what all of this means." If you're like me, you say, "Whew. Thanks. I needed that." The seed is the Word of God. With a brief understanding of first century farming, do you have a glimpse into the heart of Jesus? Remember, seeds were flung everywhere. Jesus' heart is not to keep the Kingdom from anyone, but rather He wants more people to hear and be a part of it all. He knows a lot of people will hear great news without a thought of obeying. He still wants to give a lot of people a chance. The Word is flung.

If the seed is the Word of God, then we're good to go. We've got this parable figured out. Let's move on. This parable is all about reading your Bible (sigh). I'm supposed to read my Bible more (prolonged sigh). That lessoned was drilled into me every summer at Vacation Bible School. How about you?

Ancient rabbis used to tell everybody how important it was to study scripture. Read your Bibles. Study Torah. To help emphasize their point, rabbis would create their own parables to spur people towards God's Word. Many of these parables involve "fours." One popular example put people into four comparative categories: a sponge, a funnel, a strainer, and a sieve.

Rabbis would explain how sponges soak up everything. Funnels take things in at one end, but release at the other. A strainer allows wine to pass through while keeping the dregs. A sieve is capable of straining chaff while retaining flour. Rabbis would use any means or mental images possible to challenge folks to dig deeper into the Bible. In Jesus' day, such rabbinical parables would have been abundant. Jewish people would have thought, "I'm supposed to read my Bible more (sigh). Got it." The four-types parables would have kept listeners on a constant guilt edge to read their Bibles.

Jesus gives one of His own four-types parables, but this one is different. Instead of four random kitchen utensils, Jesus creatively talks about four different kinds of dirt. Remember, dirt in the Bible is attached to life. Jesus is telling us more than just read your Bible. He's pointing to us to life... eternal life now... a relationship... if we want it.

Do you see the dirt compacted on the path Jesus pointed to? The devil is able to walk all over this path, and steal away any seeds of the Word so people can't believe or be saved.

I was enjoying one of the first glorious days of spring by bopping along in my car with the music turned up to a Spinal Tap eleven. An Amy Winehouse song came blaring on. "They try to make me go to rehab, I say no, no, no." [3] Have you heard this one? It really is catchy. With great ambivalence, I was singing along until finally my pastor filter kicked in and I thought to myself, "What am I listening to?" These top-40 lyrics captured my attention, and I rushed home for a quick Google search. Lyrically, "Rehab" is actually very dark, and doesn't seem to fit my criteria for bopping in the car. Winehouse sings about addiction, abuse, losing your kids, and all kinds of horribly real stuff. After a little research on Amy, I found out she was prone to being booed off stages because she frequently sang while being out-of-her-mind drunk. She was chronicled as being depressed and emotionally struggling with a jail-bird husband. Life was falling apart for Amy Winehouse about the time "Rehab" was rising in the charts. My judgmental side could have quickly dismissed the ridiculousness of such pop icons. I'm really good and self-righteous like that. However, with a little dirt in hand, I wondered if a person like Amy Winehouse had compacted soil. Maybe her path didn't allow seeds to grow and gave Satan easy access for stealing. Sadly, the pop singer died suddenly in July, 2011 of acute alcohol poisoning.

There might be attempts at sowing the Word, but nothing happens with hard soil. Are you starting to see why Jesus' focus on dirt is so important? Dirt is life (or not) depending on whether or not the dirt is hard and compressed. Sin is what keeps people from working their soil. It's not about mistakes or diseases or predispositions. It's about sin. S.I.N. Can we let that thought simply remain so the rationalizing pendulum can swing to a more balanced center? Gossip, cheating, lying, drunkenness, homosexuality, pornography, pastoral pride… all are sin and all keep the dirt very hard and unyielding.

What's the condition of your soil? With a little digging, some may find their dirt hard because religion has blocked the necessary nutrients. Church statisticians (a great gig if you can get it) tell us: "the probability of someone embracing Jesus as his or her savior was 32 percent for those between the ages of five and 12; four percent for those in the 13-18 range; and six percent for people 19 and older. In other words, if people do not embrace Jesus Christ as their Savior before they reach their teenage years, the chance of their doing so at all is slim."[4] People normally inject Jesus into their lives before the age of 18. Why is this? I believe it's a matter of dirt. It's a thing of soil being soft and fertile. The older we become, the harder our dirt gets. If dirt is life, Satan can effectively rob us with each passing year.

There is also seed dropping on rocks. Jesus says this compares to those who initially receive the Word with joy. There's just no available root system. There is no dirt; no life. They might believe for a while, but in difficult circumstances they fall away. I've seen so many people who show up at church for the first time and say, "Pastor, this was awesome. I'll be back." I've actually had a newbie tell me, "Pastor, this was F****ing awesome. I'll be back." I appreciate honest enthusiasm even when it's colorful. Many such excited people, however, never return. I'm always baffled. I think it's a dirt thing. The seed quickly sprang up, but there was nothing to grow in.

Jesus's continued his story telling with seed falling among unfriendly thorns. Our Lord defined this as people who allow the Word to get choked from their life. Worries, riches, pleasures, and stock portfolios tend to get in the way. Did you catch the irony? The stuff of life becomes more important than life itself. Dirt has lost its value.

Don't you see this a lot? So many aspire to life beyond God. So many could grab eternal life now, but settle for the synthetically made potting soil of temporal bling. A bigger house, shinier car, stuff that's better than the neighbors, and busier lifestyles choke any chance of the life Jesus is espousing.

Allegedly, a hurried lady pulled up to a yellow traffic light in Atlanta. If you've ever lived in this great city, you know what you're supposed to do when you come to a yellow light. You speed up. A yellow light in Atlanta is a traffic signal yelling, "Come on, hurry up and get through this!" You're supposed to give it more gas when you see yellow.

Our fateful lady was driving in Atlanta traffic, and the light turned yellow. She had a car in front of her, but the out of town lead driver put on his breaks. You can't do that in Atlanta. You will die! Our female driver was irate because she quickly calculated her 15-second delay to work. The time saved by doing make-up while driving was forever gone. She lost fifteen ticks of her life, and began cussing at the driver in front of her whose brake lights were still glowing. With great animation, she blew her horn and flipped him off with a non-southern bird. Within seconds, there was a knock on the window of her car. It was a stern-looking, stereotypical Georgia State Highway Patrol officer. The policeman instructed her to exit her car and place her hands on her head like a wanted criminal. She was being arrested. The officer read her the necessary legal rights, slapped some handcuffs on, and slammed her into the back of the patrol car. It was a short drive to the police station where they thumb printed her and threw her into a crowded, cold cell. All of this happened so very quickly. After sitting in jail for two hours, this uncorked volcano of estrogen saw the arresting policeman walk sheepishly up to her cell. He whispered, "There's been a mistake and we're releasing you." Returning to her flamboyant attitude, this female NASCAR hopeful said, "Well I would certainly think so. What in the world happened?" The officer explained, "While you were cursing, yelling, screaming, blowing your horn, and going ballistic, I noticed something. It was a sticker on the back of your car. The sticker questioned what Jesus would do. You had another bumper sticker that said 'Choose Life.' On the right side of your bumper yet another sticker instructed people to follow you to Sunday School. To complete your vehicular billboard, there was also a very prominent fish displayed. When I saw all of this I assumed this was a stolen car."

I don't think many of us intentionally set out to be like that. Most Christians start out being in love with Jesus, and thankful for eternal life now. Then our sad version of life begins to put a chokehold on us. We're forced to settle for a religion that can accommodate all our stuff and our way of life. But remember, there's life in the dirt.

When the Word of God falls on good dirt, it does four things. Rabbi Jesus goes back into the ancient methodology of "fours" (Noble, good, retaining, persevering). Jesus wants to give us a life that is light years beyond JUST reading our Bibles. He can till our soil in wonderful nobility producing ways. The Greek word for *noble* points to a life full of integrity and character. This is everything your kids need to see in you, and everything you want to be when nobody is looking. Life can be noble.

Having a good heart speaks to the activities of life. Who we are must be matched by what we do. Good dirt prompts us to be compassionate and justice-seeking for those who have been robbed of it. If you've ever given a few dollars to that homeless man with a cardboard sign, you know how good this feels. The spiritual endorphins coming from such compassionate giving are miniscule glimpses of what all of life should look like if we pay attention to the dirt.

Good soil allows the Word of God to be retained. That may sound like we're going backwards to "just read your Bible." That's not what's going on here. Please don't sigh, again, just yet.

Biblically, the Word is synonymous with Jesus. Jesus is the Bible and the Bible is Jesus. The book of John gives us a wonderful mystery of our faith. *"In the beginning was the Word and the Word was God and the Word was with God and the word became flesh."* (John 1:1) Jesus is the Word. The Word is Jesus. The Bible you may have sitting next to you is not a book to simply read and study. This is a relationship to develop. This is the kind of dirt --- and life --- Jesus is promoting, promising, and wanting to live out inside you. The good dirt relates to a person who applies, understands, and retains the Word. This person also has a relational yearning for Jesus. This kind of person yields a bumper crop; a hundred fold. Again, that's farmer talk for a lot.

The New Testament book of Mark includes this same "Play in the Dirt Again" parable. Mark is the parallel gospel writer giving the idea of a 100-fold crop. In the ancient Middle East, you were rockin' if you had a 10% increase in your harvest. If you had a 20% jump, you were richly blessed. An increase of 30% with your harvest was unheard of. In Jesus' day, a literal 100-fold crop would take them back several thousand years to Abraham. Abraham had it all, baby. A nation out-numbering the grains of sand on the beach came from Abraham. It was a supernatural life only God could have created. Abraham was the one "biggie" hero Jewish people would attach to such a miraculous bounty.

If your life has a 100%, 100-fold crop, then God is doing supernatural things nobody can explain. Beyond your wildest dreams or imagination, God will do things that are flat out amazing... according to His Spirit working inside of you (Ephesians 3:20). Are you intrigued by that prospect? I am.

Why aren't there more *Christians* who are experiencing the mind boggling, 100-fold life? Why do so many believers remain unsure if they can even trust God? Too many still have unresolved verdicts bout God's goodness and put Him neatly in a box that settles for stale religion. There's no life.

Shouldn't there be more churches seeing 100% increases in their harvest? Current church growth gurus explain a 10% rise is more than adequate. Have we settled?

Mike Yaconelli was a great writer, author, and very eccentric pastor. He tragically died in 2003. Yaconelli left us with many real-life stories, including the one about how cows get lost. In California, cows easily get lost. Golden Staters are often baffled as to why. Are the cows stupid, or are the farmers irresponsible? Why do cows get lost? Mike Yaconelli decided to figure out the science behind lost California cows.

He spoke to a local farmer. An overall-wearing and slow speaking lover of dirt told Yaconelli cows don't really mean to get lost. The cows aren't bad. It's not like they intentionally set out to get lost, but here is what happens: Cows move away from their home barns with their heads down eating tufts of grass. Once their heads are down, they move from tuft to tuft until they are stuffed. Tuft to tuft and stuffed. Without looking up, cows will move further and further away with only the next patch of grass in their sights. Before you know it, they are two miles down the road and completely lost.[4]

I still believe people are good, even those boxy *Christians* this book seems to malign. Most people don't intentionally set out to be lost in a compacted religion. I can't name one person who says, "I want religion. I don't want life." Most people would check the box that says, "I want eternal life now." Do you know of anyone who would put a checkmark in the other box that says, "I don't want a relationship; I want my God in a box?"

Here's what happens: We slowly move from one worry of life to the next. With heads down in the weeds and thorns, we methodically take on the stuff of a distorted life. We get all choked up. We slowly let sin creep in. We slowly give Satan permission to rob us of life. We never set out to be lost, but here we stand with a weakening label of *Christian* to define our anemic efforts.

We've drifted, but Jesus is holding out a handful of soil and wants to know if we will play in the dirt again.

What do we do? Some have very hard soil. Maybe the Word of God has never been able to be planted. If this is you, do you feel God's hand beginning to do some plowing? Will you allow Him?

Maybe God is stirring and you know the apparition of religion is an extremely slippery slope. You've tried your brand of religion or *Christianity*, and it's left you wanting. You may be completely done with church. All the religious peripherals once deemed important and necessary are not now. There still is dirt for you to play in again. There is eternal life now that Jesus is offering. Jesus didn't die on a cross so you could have *religion* stamped on your forehead. Rather, He offers a noble, good, retaining, and persevering life. Now.

Some are beyond ready to accept all of this. You are done with being helplessly choked out of life. You want what Jesus offers. Eternal life now. You want the vitality of a supernatural relationship. Dirt. There's life in the dirt Jesus is holding out to you.

Will you give me the grace and space to close this chapter with a brief prayer for you and me?

"Jesus, in these moments, help us to listen to You. Supercharge our hunger for You. Give us a palpable distaste for religion. Please bring us to a point of complete exhaustion of the life-sapping effects of religion. I pray for a fresh glimpse of what a relationship with You would look like. Jesus, You are offering us eternal life now. Help us to grab onto that. Help us to consider the soil of our lives and the life You want to give us. Thanks, Jesus, for dying on the cross. Thanks for wanting us to have such a life. Thank You for Your sacrifice. God, we're sorry when we take the love and sacrifice of Jesus and stuff it into our presumptuous religious boxes. Forgive us. Get us out of those boxes right now. Help us to decide right now. In Jesus' name we pray, Amen."

Chapter End Notes

1. William P. Young, The Shack, (Windblown Media, 2007), 204-205.
2. Swindoll, Living on the Ragged Edge, p. 37.
3. Amy Winehouse, Album: Back to Black, Universal Republic, 2006
4. George Barna, Transforming Children into Spiritual Champions (provenance: Regal Books, 2003), 34.
5. Mike Yaconelli, The Wittenburg Door, Fall 1988.

Chapter Seven

Storms Are For Sisters

Strategy #7: Learn how to navigate storms.

Luke 8:22-25

"One day Jesus said to his disciples, "Let's go over to the other side of the lake." So they got into a boat and set out. As they sailed, he fell asleep. A squall came down on the lake, so that the boat was being swamped, and they were in great danger. The disciples went and woke him, saying, "Master, Master, we're going to drown!" He got up and rebuked the wind and the raging waters; the storm subsided, and all was calm. "Where is your faith?" he asked his disciples. In fear and amazement they asked one another, "Who is this? He commands even the winds and the water, and they obey him."

How's your luck with storms? Ever wrestled a tornado? In 1974 I tried. I managed to pile a lifetime's worth of storms in one memorable experience. Having turned 14, I was dealing with mom and dad's nasty divorce. It was bad. Outside my formative Ohio house, the storm clouds were gathering. Inside a squall was brewing on the phone as I bantered with dad. I remember brutally verbalizing how Dad just didn't seem to care. He seemed very much alive to a mid-life crisis, but oblivious to what was happening in the hearts of his family. Suddenly, the phone line went eerily dead.

My frantic mother came running from the upstairs and into the kitchen where I was holding a dead phone. Mom yelled, "Alan, get to the basement now!" She grabbed my eight-year-old sister, and we sprinted to a basement corner. At this point, things in my mind begin to move in a very deliberate slow motion. As we ran across the basement carpet, windows began to pop just behind us. One at a time… pop, Pop, POP… they blew out as we made our way to the safety of a corner.

For some ten years later, my younger sister would nose dive underneath the kitchen table any time a dark cloud would form. In fact, strong winds or a clap of ominous thunder still sound internal alarms for my sis. That's the kind of real trauma our storm caused. My sister, Lynn, carries emotional scars, which tend to resurface when inclement weather flashes warnings across the bottom of the TV screen. On the other hand my older brother, Greg, went largely unscarred. He was sitting naively upstairs in his bed not paying attention to the subtle sounds of a freight train busting through our house. Somewhere in the chaos of Mother Nature's fury, a 2x4 from the neighbor's house torpedoed through the dark air. It pierced Greg's bedroom wall stopping only inches away from his head. This shook him slightly, but a few days afterwards he began to view his providential care as "far out." It was the 70's. Unlike my sister, the tornado was no big deal for my 17-year-old, big brother.

Any chance you're going through a storm of your own right now? The Weather Channel may be predicting clear skies, but your storm is undeniable. Perhaps the daunting trauma has you under the table with debilitating fear. Maybe you've become storm-callused, and another bout is no big deal. Nonetheless, there are financial storms, job hurricanes, marital blizzards, parental downpours, typhoons of divorce, tempests of death, and health tsunamis. The circumstantial evidence is mounting. Yep, you're smack dab in the middle of a doozy.

Sometimes it feels like God is unaware. Almost like an estranged Father on the other end of a dead phone, it seems as if God is asleep at the wheel. It feels like He just stopped caring... especially when the winds start to kick in. I know people who have been through many storms. It's almost become a way of life. Strangely, people begin fueling their lives with crisis after crisis. Still, they're not sure they can actually take on more water or endure another flying 2x4.

More and more people these days are coming to church with drenched spiritual raincoats. They're looking for help to ride out the storm. Becoming victorious would be great, but just surviving would be, at this point, OK too.

I've employed a deliberate parenting strategy with my three oldest daughters, Brooklynn, Lauren, & Morgan. It's a bit of a premeditated storm. Perhaps you're familiar with this technique. A dubious attempt to educate through intentional displacement is my turbulent objective. I subject my kids to the traumatic social horrors of currency exchange in the real world. I force my girls to place an order by facing an actual human on the other side of the counter at Chick-Fil-A. They must speak clearly, hand over the money, wait for the change, and finish with a strong thank you. That's the drill. Each time my girls are subjected to such outlandish parenting there is a public freaking out. There is wailing and teeth gnashing of Biblical proportions. My daughters could only wonder why their father makes them go through such a painful exercise.

When you're trying to teach your kids, what's one of the absolute best arenas for learning? You throw them right into the fire, don't you? You give them just enough rope to survive exactly because you love them. You know they've got to grow and learn to stand on their own two feet. An eagle as a parent is no different. When a mom eagle is trying to get the little ones to fly, she starts bringing painful thorns and thistles into the nest. This makes life a bit uncomfortable. It gets worse. Eventually the matriarchal eagle just boots her children out of the nest and off the cliff to hopefully fly... exactly because she loves them.

Would you like a deeper faith? Aren't you reading this book because you're hoping to go beyond the impotence of what *Christian* has become? How might a Heavenly Father deepen your faith? How would a Heavenly Father push us to be more like Jesus?

Jesus worked and prayed to deepen the faith of friends closest to him. As a rabbi, Jesus had several followers. Officially they were called disciples or talmidim. They followed Jesus very closely. By closely, I mean there would literally be scrambling to see who would have the best proximity to Jesus. Followers of ancient rabbis believed the more their clothes were caked with the dust and dirt from the heels of a rabbi, the more glory they would claim as a disciple. The more dirt your white button-down boasted, the closer you were to your heralded rabbi.

One day, Jesus tells His jockeying disciples He wants to sail to the opposite side of a lake. There is a place He had to go. There is purpose and intent with the course He's plotting. Enthusiastically, Jesus' disciples jump into the boat and head out. I'm not sure anyone caught a glimpse of the ominous storm clouds gathering. Is it possible Jesus would take His friends right into the middle of a storm? Is that Biblical? Is that… right?

Some pastors commanding the podium and say, "If you're having difficulties, if there are storms in your life, then there is no God in your life." Personally, I think such preaching is bogus. You have to be very careful with such reasoning. The first-century, Jewish people believed if you were experiencing storms of disease or financial difficulties, there was sin in your life. Such ancient thinking is highlighted in the Old Testament book of Job.

Job had massive thunderhead storms, and his closest friends questioned, "What did you do? What sin did you commit?" Here's the truth to this. Although it wasn't the case for Job, you CAN experience storms because of poor decision making, stupidity, and sin. Former governor of New York, Eliot Spitzer, is evidence. His political career came crashing down after he bought a $43,000 hooker. That was sin AND stupid! Sin and stupidity cause storms in your life.

The decisions of People around you can cause very real storms for you to maneuver. I'm sure you've had to deal with other people's severe weather forecast problems. However, here is an additional truth you must know as well. If you consider yourself as a close follower or disciple of Rabbi Jesus, you should grasp this proven fact: Sometimes He will lead you into a storm. Why would He do this? It's exactly because He loves you and wants to develop your faith. Jesus will never take you into dangerous, deeper waters to drown you. He will take you there to develop you. Put that on your next refrigerator magnet.

Consider this *Christian* platitude: "The safest place to be is in the center of God's will." Have you heard that one? It sounds really warm and fuzzy, doesn't it? It might make for a good, decorative, Christian coffee mug, but I'm not sure I would drink from it. Most comfort-seeking Christians believe this sappy sentiment to be true. Safety and the center of God's will are hoped to be synonymous. It's Biblically wrong. The testimony of serious disciples over the years will prove the fallacy of such bad theology. Often times, the closer you are to Jesus, the more dangerous life can become. Why on earth would God operate as such? He's developing you. He's pushing you out of His comfortable nest in hopes you'll fly. All the while, Satan is scratching, clawing, and fighting too. Those become the components of a perfect storm.

Within our storms there are spiritual realities and things unseen we need to grab onto. To open our eyes a bit more, we need to ruminate on what life would be like without difficulties. Can you imagine the emotional, mental, spiritual, and physical atrophy plaguing our kids if there were no dark clouds? I can't imagine the outcome of my kids' lives if we all moved into the perfect world of Disney Land. What if their diet consisted of only Disney Land food? What if my children's only challenges were the occasional long lines? Three words would aptly describe what my children would quickly morph into: Dumbo, Dopey, and Goofy. If I tried to afford a life that was a piece of cake, my kid's icing would assuredly melt in the scorching sun of the real world. What if life with God was a proverbial piece of cake? What kind of people would we be molded into? Here are a few words to attach to such a life: self-centered, empty, weak, one-dimensional, and very, very shallow. As much as we might despise them, it looks as if we need storms. So how should we respond when the driving rain begins to erase our visibility?

Jesus sets sail with His friends, and He falls asleep in the back of the boat. Why did Jesus fall asleep? There is something subtle yet profoundly eye-opening going on. Jesus is God, but He also exudes a very real dose of humanity. On the human side of things, Jesus has been teaching His brains out. He's tired. Jesus has been dealing with thousands of sick, needy people. He is headed to another purposeful event, but a nap in the boat is the most spiritual thing He can do. He lets His friends take the helm, while

He takes a snooze. That is the reality of the physical, human side of things. There is divinity and God-stuff oozing, but Jesus sleeps with some very cool humanness.

A storm begins to brew. A squall quickly hits the water. The boat carrying God starts to rock and roll. It starts to take on water. Even God's boat starts to take on water! Why do I get so puzzled and befuddled when mine does?

Jesus's friends notice the dirt from their rabbi washing off as the wind and rain throws them all into a spin cycle. In a moment of sheer panic, someone yells, "Master, Master, we're going to drown!" Jesus does an interrupted nap stretch, rebukes the storm (I love that), and brings peace like a glassy river.

It would be good to grab onto a little background at this point. This storm took place on the Sea of Galilee. Refresh your memory. It's a large lake about 13 miles long, and five to seven miles wide. Uniquely, this body of water is 700 feet below sea level. The beauty of the Sea of Galilee is punctuated by the very grand mountains wrapping around its shores. When crisp, cool winds come blowing through the mountains and ravines, they can hit warm water and cause storms to pop up without much warning. These outbursts can be immediate and very dangerous.

Are you thinking Jesus's friends are boating weenies? After all, Dr. Luke says its only a squall. Most of Jesus's sailing buddies are, however, weathered, salty, fisherman. They have fished the Sea of Galilee plenty of times before. These disciples of

Rabbi Jesus have been in storms before. This one is different.

This same story is also found in the books of Matthew and Mark. Matthew uses a word that can mean either tornado or earthquake. It can also point to a tsunami. For seasoned experts who understand the temperament of the Sea of Galilee, this is something they have never seen. This is why they were freaking out. This is why they believe they are going to die.

Take note of how all three parallel stories record the responses of Jesus' friends. Matthew, Mark, and Luke all record different cries of panic. This is a rollercoaster ride of emotions worn on the sleeves and fishing nets of those in God's boat. "Lord, save us. We're going to drown." This is clearly a cry for help. "Master, Master, we're going to drown!" This is a blunt factual statement of doom. We ARE going to die. Mark records, "Teacher, don't You care if we drown?" This one reflects a bit of an attitude towards their rabbi for sleeping.

If you're questioning which of these statements was actually said, the answer is *yes*. All three were vocalized in the middle of the storm. We say similar things when sunny skies turn dark. I've blurted those same cries of help, doom, and attitude. If you do the same, then you and I (along with Jesus' disciples) are very much human. It's a natural way to respond when circumstances feel unnatural. You can make a great argument that it's Biblical to respond this way. I need help. I'm going to die. God, why are You asleep?

My graying goatee grants me permission to remember a song by Gordon Lightfoot. For some, this is really bustin' through the cranial cobwebs. One of Lightfoot's best efforts was a song called, "The Wreck of the Edmund Fitzgerald."

In 1975, a freighter ship called "The Edmund Fitzgerald" set sail on Lake Superior and found itself in the death grip of a huge storm. Gordon Lightfoot penned this great line: "Does anyone know where the love of God goes when the waves turn the minutes to hours?"[1]

Haven't you felt what Lightfoot captured? On the clock, your storm may engulf a relatively short span of time. Inside, however, the storm has been brewing for extremely long hours, days, and weeks. Your soul questions where the love of God is now. But God can handle your humanness. He's placed Himself in the middle of storms so He could understand yours. The cross of Jesus is proof.

What do you do with your fears before, during, and after the exhaustive gathering of dark clouds? There's a key point in Luke's tornado story to help with our fears.

Jesus calms the storm. It all subsides with only His words. There is so much power in His words. Jesus then asks His jaw-drooping disciples, "Where is your faith?" With what tone do you think Jesus says that? Grandfatherly? Sleepily? Calmly? Does he speak with a Donald Trump, "you're-fired" attitude? Is there some of that Old Testament fire in His voice?

Jesus severely chides the storm, and He asks His friends about their faith. I think Jesus does both with an attitude. Remember, Jesus is not only God; He is human. He was in a deep sleep. This was a well deserved, wipe the drool, over-due nap. As a nine-year-old, I wouldn't have even thought about waking up my flat-topped, hard-working father from his Sunday afternoon nap. It would have been a colorful display of wrath awakened; great to catch on video, but not so much live and in person.

For Jesus, the real problem is happening on the inside of His followers, and not on the outside of the boat. It isn't the storm that disturbs Jesus as much as His friend's lack of faith demonstrated in fear. Fear is the problem, not the storm. Fear is the struggle. Faith is the solution. Fear paralyzes faith every time.

In his book *'93*, Victor Hugo talked about a ship on the high seas getting rocked back and forth into oblivion. The storm itself was a really serious thing, but the most serious detail of the storm was happening deep inside the hull of the ship. More serious than the mountainous waves outside was what was happening inside with cast iron cannons having not been latched down. On the outside were waves and winds. On the inside there were loose cannons banging back and forth and ripping through walls. The sinking problem was on the inside![2]

Jesus is not disturbed by the storm. He is most concerned about what's going on inside the people He loves. When our power rabbi asks, ""Where is your faith?" He uses the Greek word *pistis*. Pistis means confidence. Jesus wants to know why they threw their confidence overboard.

Are you confused yet? If you're in a storm and you think you're going to die, shouldn't you wake up the Savior? Doesn't that seem logical? Why then is

Jesus asking where their confidence has gone? Is it possible Jesus is asking why THEY don't calm the storm?

Think about that. Why don't His disciples rebuke the Doppler radar? Jesus had previously told them if they had a dose of faith the size of a mustard seed (a miniscule, almost invisible thing), they could move mountains into the seas (Matthew 17:20). Where is their faith? Where is mine? Why can't I seem to hold out even a Chiclet size piece of faith?

This is all so much easier for me to write than to live. Fear grips me with great efficiency. It can give me anxiety attacks at 2 in the morning. Fear creates jacked up, mental scenarios in my surrounding relationships. These would be absolutely horrific if they were in any way true. Where does my faith go? Where is my confidence? Better still, where can I find it? How can I regain my confidence? I desperately want faith. I'm tired of the waves pounding me.

"Consequently, faith comes from hearing the message, and the message is heard through the word of Christ." (Romans 19:17) I love it when the Bible spells out things clearly. Previously I've mentioned how the Bible pointed to a relationship gained, and not simply a book to be studied. Jesus and The Word are synonymous. In the beginning was the Word. The Word was with God. The Word became flesh. The Word was God. Jesus is the Word. The Word is Jesus (John 1:1). According to the Bible writer, Paul, this is how we restore our faith and confidence.

So why have we replaced the words of Jesus with the words of Oprah? When Oprah speaks, millions follow. She enthusiastically touted a book called *A Course in Miracles*. This best-seller claimed several things: There is no sin; a slain Christ has no meaning; do not make the pathetic error of clinging to The Old Rugged Cross; the name of Jesus, as such, is but a symbol; it is a symbol that is safely used as a replacement for the many names of all the gods to which you pray; the recognition of God is the recognition of yourself; the oneness of the Creator and the creation is your wholeness, your sanity, and your limitless power. Oprah, and subsequent millions, thought *A Course in Miracles* replaced sliced bread and the words of Jesus.

What do you think happens when a *Christian* replaces the Word of God with the words of the latest self-help crap? When a hurricane comes ashore, isn't it reasonable to assume we would fall apart without a trace of faith or Godly confidence? Have you discovered how Oprah's and other guru words only work when skies are clear? When a storm hits, fear takes up residence. Confidence hits the road. Maybe fear should be a warning flare to illuminate the dark words we've allowed to replace the words of Jesus.

Many Christian gathering spots have neglected the words of Jesus to the point most evangelical American churches rarely open their Bibles. We have become a Biblically illiterate America. When we hit storms, we're crushed. We can't understand why fear has gripped us. We've lost our faith. Our confidence is shot. Why? Because faith comes from hearing the Word, and so many just aren't listening.

Neither were the disciples. Being good Jewish boys, Jesus' followers should have been all over Psalm 107. They should have remembered. This Old Testament passage is about a ship in a storm! The writer penned these faith launching words, *"They reeled and staggered like drunken men; they were at their wits' end. Then they cried out to the Lord in their trouble, and He brought them out of their distress. He stilled the storm to a whisper; the waves of the sea were hushed."* Sound familiar? Application of the Word in their Sea of Galilee storm would have allowed faith to prevail and fear to be squelched.

Here are words for your storm: *"Cast all your anxiety on Him because He cares for you."* (I Peter 5:7) When driving rain is dousing your faith, cast your nets of fear on God. Give it up. Feeling fear? Throw it on God. He cares. He can take it. He can handle it. Going back to the Word builds up faith and chases fear out the portal. Do you see how this can work?

I remember my parents teaching me a great mealtime prayer. It started off with, "God is great, God is good." What a concise (especially if you're really hungry) prayer to pray. Mom and Dad were pointing to great scripture passages with that prayer. Psalm 145 is just one example of the idea "God is great, God is good."

Want a good prayer for your tornado twisting and destroying your confidence? Try this one, "God is great, God is good." We've relegated this to a happy meal prayer. It's nonetheless spiritual and scriptural truth. Say it out loud. "God is great, God is good." Say it every morning. Repeat it at night when your head hits the pillow. No matter the weather forecast, God is great and God is good. Say it until you begin living it. I have a friend who knows the real meaning of "starving artist" and what the top of the Grammy-hungry music world is like. Kuk often throws at me, "God is great, so whatever!" I love that.

One last storm-related thought. Could storms be more about other folks and not your obvious pain? Could our storms have a purpose beyond us?

After Jesus chastised the tsunami and His friends, dry ground was welcomed on the other side of the lake. They made it to a place called Gerasenes. It was where Jesus had intended to land all along. Remember when they began their cruise? Jesus wanted to go to the other side of the Sea of Galilee. It seemed He had a place to go. He had a purpose for boarding the boat besides grabbing a little shuteye. What was destined to happen on the other side of lake at Gerasenes? There was a demon-possessed man there who needed God. He needed healing. He needed ministered to. He longed for friends once again. Did Jesus decide His friends must go through the storm, deepen their faith, and develop themselves SO THAT they would be able to help this demon-possessed man?

It's entirely within the scope of eternal possibilities that your storm is not about you. God may be developing you, deepening you, and dealing with you exactly because somebody somewhere needs your help. God is about to show His love and grace to someone through you. Those storms we get so self-absorbed in (*why me, why me, why me?*) may not be about us. Perhaps they're more about somebody else. You OK with that?

That little sister of mine grew up. You remember, the one whose mailing address was legally changed to say "under the kitchen table." When Lynn was 17, she married a guy by the name of Joe Bennett. Joe was a charismatic evangelist. He was a traveling singer/preacher who trekked the country. My parents gave my under-aged sister their approval to marry Joe because, in their words, "He's such a good guy. He's Godly. Yes, yes, yes... get married!" They did.

Joe and Lynn's first year of marriage was spent traveling from coast to coast doing revivals, concerts, and preaching good news of Jesus's Kingdom wherever they could. About three months into the marriage, Joe and Lynn were driving across the plains of Kansas. Their van and trailer hit a vicious crosswind. Everything was wiped out. All equipment, clothes, and belongings were lost in a tailwind of bad insurance.

Eight months into their very young marriage, a squall blew in. An unfortunate miscarriage had to be battled through. Then, on the one-year anniversary of Lynn and Joe's whirlwind marriage, our family received crushing news of Joe's serious blood disorder called A-plastic Anemia. My sister had just turned 18.

A-plastic Anemia is a devastating blood disease with platelet counts so low the blood can't coagulate any longer. White cells are depleted, and immune systems go completely south. You can't cut yourself shaving or catch a common cold without the very real threat of dying when A-plastic Anemia is your battle.

Joe courageously dealt with this horrific disease for another full year. He was in and out of the hospital with blood transfusions, platelet transfusions, and a desperate bone marrow transplant. At the end of that very trying year, Joe died. He was 26, and my younger sister was 19. She was a widow at 19. The thought still stops me dead in my tracks.

This was quite a wild ride for my entire family. The funeral was touted as a victory celebration. Joe's dad preached the funeral sermon. His mom played the piano, while Joe's grandfather somehow managed to lead on the organ. Grand old hymns like "Onward Christian Solders" were sung with resounding spiritual determination.

We buried the lifeless shell of Joe in the afternoon. That evening several friends and family members drove 20 minutes to Rehoboth Beach, Delaware. The water and boardwalk there became one of Joe and Lynn's favorite spots to refresh. As several of us walked down to the beach, we were greeted with a bright, red sun sinking slowly into the dark ocean. Somebody said out loud, "Come now, Lord Jesus. We're ready. We're tired. Just come."

After an awkward pause, another friend rightfully said, "Why don't we pray?" We circled up and did just that. We held hands and I started the prayer circle. Everybody prayed really short prayers. They were nervous prayers stemming from funeral weary folks with nothing profound to say. As it happened, my sister was the last to pray. I will never forget her words. In a whisper barely heard over the crashing waves, Lynn prayed, "Thanks for Jesus. How does anybody make it without Him?"

In the middle of her storm, she was able to do the God is great and God is good thing. In the eye of the hurricane, Lynn somehow found her way to praise. She was able to worship. Incredible.

Fast forward things ten years, and you'd find Lynn married to another pastor. She's a glutton for punishment! Lynn and Scott have two great kids and they've planted a thriving church in Clarksville, Tennessee.

Recently I visited Lynn, and went to church with her family. She was on stage leading worship with such a powerful and direct line to God. I saw so many people connecting with her. There were people being baptized. People were being saved all over that place. These external sights began flooding my soul and I couldn't help but offer up a brief, conversational prayer. I prayed something like, "Wow, God, You must really love lost people to take my sister through a crazy-difficult storm so that she could eventually minister to these people in Tennessee. God, You must really love these southern people to allow my sister to go through a second tornado."

That's how much God loves us. That's how much He loves people who are far, far, far away from Him. As Christians, we'd better be ready to go through a storm understanding that it might be about somebody else. If this should happen, will you have the ability, like my sister, to praise Him in that very same storm?

Some are not connected to Jesus. If this is you, with penetrating maturity my sister would look you squarely in the eyes and ask, "How do you make it?"

How are you going to make it? How will you resolve to replace fear with faith? Will you replace self-help words with Jesus'? In order to regain the influence and credibility as a card-carrying *Christian*, it seems we must learn to praise Him in the inevitable storms. Maybe there's somebody on the other side of the lake waiting.

Chapter End Notes

1. Gordon Lightfoot, <u>Summer Time Dream</u>. 1976, Reprise
2. Victor Hugo, <u>Ninety-Three</u>, (Boston, New York, The Jefferson Press, 1908)

Chapter Eight

Power Problem

Strategy #8: Stop settling.

Luke 8:40-56

"Now when Jesus returned, a crowd welcomed him, for they were all expecting him. Then a man named Jairus, a ruler of the synagogue, came and fell at Jesus' feet, pleading with him to come to his house because his only daughter, a girl of about twelve, was dying.

As Jesus was on his way, the crowds almost crushed him. And a woman was there who had been subject to bleeding for twelve years, but no one could heal her. She came up behind him and touched the edge of his cloak, and immediately her bleeding stopped.

"Who touched me?" Jesus asked. When they all denied it, Peter said, "Master, the people are crowding and pressing against you." But Jesus said, "Someone touched me; I know that power has gone out from me." Then the woman, seeing that she could not go unnoticed, came trembling and fell at his feet. In the presence of all the people, she told why she had touched him and how she had been instantly healed. Then he said to her, "Daughter, your faith has healed you. Go in peace." While Jesus was still speaking, someone came from the house of Jairus, the synagogue ruler. "Your daughter is dead," he said. "Don't bother the teacher any more." Hearing this, Jesus said to

Jairus, "Don't be afraid; just believe, and she will be healed." When he arrived at the house of Jairus, he did not let anyone go in with him except Peter, John and James, and the child's father and mother. Meanwhile, all the people were wailing and mourning for her. "Stop wailing," Jesus said. "She is not dead but asleep." They laughed at him, knowing that she was dead. But he took her by the hand and said, "My child, get up!" Her spirit returned, and at once she stood up. Then Jesus told them to give her something to eat. Her parents were astonished, but he ordered them not to tell anyone what had happened."

At times my struggle with power gets the best of me. Turning the ignition key and getting nuttin' can bring my day to a grinding halt. Most times my battery has died. There was one instance where my battery was OK, but the terminals were corroded. Embarrassingly, a stranger poured a can of Coke on the corrosion, and my car cranked right up. Who knew a simple can of soda could restore power? I took a celebrative swig from my bright red can. Those secret and guarded ingredients began eating away at the corrosion on my liver.

Recently I caught a classic episode of Seinfeld. It was the one where Jerry couldn't resist saying an annoying "Hello!" Given the choice between his girlfriend or the ability to keep saying "Heeeellllo," Jerry dumped his girlfriend. In the middle of my comedic break, Jerry and our cable went dead. It was another power problem.

With nothing to watch, I decided to turn my sad couch diving into a 30-minute run. I ran with great abandonment as my winter-washed legs blinded the oncoming traffic. My iPod was pumping some old-school Chicago. I seem to run faster when "25-Or-6-To-4" is ringing in my head. Suddenly my music went dead. I had forgotten to charge my stupid iPod. Although only halfway through my run, it was abruptly over. I hung my head and walked back home. I was defeated. Powerless.

You've experienced power problems too. They can happen in your career. They happen with relationships, finances, health, and in church world. How do you handle life when the lights go out? Settling has become a popular way of dealing with power outages. People decide there is nothing they can do to solve their problems. This resolve leads to a lowered bar of expectations and a beginning of mere existing. I know of many marriages that have also settled into a draining co-existence. No zip. No romance. No power.

An elderly couple was living out their eighties, and took a first trip to the holy land. Upon arriving in Jerusalem, the wife tragically died. The gracious residents of Jerusalem told the husband, "Listen, there are two things you can do. You can spend $5,000 and ship your wife home, or you can bury her here in Jerusalem for $150. Which would you like to do?" The sudden widower said, "I'm going to spend the $5,000 and ship her home." A bewildered group of Jewish folks couldn't believe this older gentleman would opt for the more expensive solution. They asked why. Without hesitation, the 80+ year-old husband responded. "A long time ago there was a guy who died in Jerusalem. After three days He came back to life. I can't take that chance!"[1]

We settle for less in our marriages. That's what power problems do. Maureen Dowd wrote, "When we decide to settle, we get less than what we settled for."[2] I know exactly what she means.

When Sherry and I first moved to Atlanta, our first house demanded new carpet. We took a short drive to the carpet Mecca of Dalton, Georgia. In Dalton, we stumbled into a place called Troy's. Troy's had the biggest sign and best prices. Cheesy carpet marketing totally sucked me in.

Troy's prices were a thing of romance for a cheap pastor like myself. We found a once-in-a-lifetime deal on a roll of Berber. We had to have it NOW. Sometimes there is a tendency to settle when we have to have something now. I had to have the Berber carpet.

Two days later it was installed all throughout our house, and quickly began unraveling in less than a week. We went begrudgingly back to Troy's. Negotiations and some minor league legal action ensued. There was a portion of our money returned, but we had to pay our carpet installer twice once we finally found good carpet. When you settle for less, you get less than you settled for. Sherry and I lost money, and Troy's Carpet eventually went out of business. The darkness within feels vindicated writing those words of demise. I feel semi-powerful.

Our tendency is to settle for less when there is less power. Why are we like that? The Bible advocates the exact opposite.

God begins His journey with us by promoting mankind to a position of power and dominance. Adam and Eve were told to be fruitful, increase, rule, and subdue. Before the introduction of sin, ruling and subduing were the order of the day. How many of us will have epitaphs boasting of bold ruling and subduing?

Jesus confidently claims that we will be doing greater things than He did. Some of you are laughing at that one. The Apostle Paul was a man of power who had several muscle sound bytes: *"I can do everything through Him who gives me strength."* (Philippians 4:13) *"I want to know Christ and the power of His resurrection."* (Philippians 3:10)

For some settlers, the Bible teeters on the ridiculous when it claims power. The power which, raised Jesus from the dead, is the same power that can pulse through our veins (Romans 8:11). Resurrection power is available. God willingly laid down His own life only to raise it back up again. That amazing power is offered to you and me, but not too many are inking the deal.

Some Christian settlers only want an image of Godliness, but not the power (II Timothy 3:5). The Bible has harsh recommendations for those who go through the religious motions, wear bright pastels and pasted smiles on Easter. Such folks have no grasp on the power of God. According to the Bible, those kinds of Christians are to be left alone by those who are trying to follow Jesus. Wow. Maybe we'd better sort through this whole power problem.

God's standard for power is the resurrection, and that's where we have to start. Somebody once said, "God showed His love through the cross, but He shows His power through the resurrection." With a cautionary style, Jim Cymbala explains in his excellent book, "Fresh Power," how when Christians get together and go to church, they start talking about power. They usually go to two extremes. One extreme is the insane asylum where we get all crazy about power. The other extreme is when we don't think there's any more available, and we're stuck in cemeteries.[3]

Do you remember one of the beginning scenes in Bruce Almighty when Jim Carrey discovers his God powers? He lets it fly with the point of a finger --- all to the music of "I've Got the Power." There's actually a fair slice of believers who try to go nuts with God's gracious gift of power. Should they go in the insane asylum? Most times, I tend to think so. I'm confident that's a very bad attitude on my part. I can't seem to forget Mark Driscoll, pastor of Mars Hill Church in Seattle, praying, "Lord, could you please rapture the charismatic lady who brings her tambourine to church?"[4] Meanwhile, others slant in the opposite direction and deny any semblance of God possibilities. A church full of those folks makes a cemetery look like an amusement park.

Sorting through this power problem, Dr. Luke points us to a specific story involving Jesus. After a successful return from sailing and taming a tsunami, Jesus confronts two desperate people. One is a tired parent of a sick child. The other is sick and tired.

News of Jesus's clout is gaining quite a following for the self-proclaimed Messiah. It seems everyone wants a piece of His miracle action. Crowds of desperate people bring gut-wrenching stories to the feet of Jesus, literally. One story involves Jairus, a local director of a Jewish Synagogue. His daughter has just been put on life support. Jairus is a desperate father at the end of solutions. His humble pleading is proof of his desperation.

Synagogues were ancient Jewish community centers. Wedding, funerals, teaching, meals, and much of life took place there. Jairus, as a leader of the synagogue, is tied into the religious elite of the extremely Jewish landscape. The religious elite are the ones who hate Jesus. They reject Jesus's claim as the long-awaited Messiah, and they want Him dead. Jairus' falling at the feet of Jesus would seriously be throwing things like caution, job security, and reputation to the wind. He no longer cares what his churchy cronies think. He has a seriously sick little girl. Jesus may be his only hope.

As a dad, I can recount many times when the kids were very little and very sick. Late night hospital runs would take precedence over any deadlines or projects waiting at the office. Running red lights on the way to emergency rooms was something not thought twice about. When your child is sick, you don't care about laws, your job, your reputation, or what anyone else may think. If you understand this, you understand Jairus.

Years ago I dealt with a family whose only child had cystic fibrosis. This bright-eyed, blonde-haired daughter was being treated at Emory Children's Center in Atlanta. The sick child was 22. Life expectancy of a kid with cystic fibrosis is normally between 25 and 30. When you looked at the parents' eyes, you saw desperation. You heard their desperation when you heard their prayers. There's a correlation between desperation and power. Our point of desperation seems to move the very hand of God. When we're at the end of a medical rope, often times God's power begins to be displayed. If you have a need for God's power, you must consider your desperation quotient.

As Jesus is on His way to help Jairus, the curious and the hurting begin invading Jesus's space. Have you ever been in such close quarters the thought of suffocation crossed your mind? When I was eight years old, my dad took me to a Cincinnati Reds game at old Crosley Field. It was a packed ballpark. The ensuing rain delay made the outing almost unbearable. Holding on to my dad's hand, we headed for shelter. That's where my trauma began. I can recall it all so quickly. Being eight years old, I was nipping at everybody's knees. The air I was sucking on smelled of stale beer, hot dogs, peanuts, and rain. I felt like I couldn't breathe. A panic began to set in. I knew I would suffocate and never see Pete Rose again. This is the kind of crowding Jesus is navigating in our story.

In the middle of the chaotic mob, a woman touches Jesus. She has been bleeding for 12 years. This is more than likely a female, gynecological type bleeding. The books of Matthew and Mark repeat this story and tell how this poor woman has spent all of her money on doctors. Nobody could help her. Why doesn't Luke mention this little tidbit? It's because Luke is a doctor himself. He doesn't want to rip on his own profession. That almost unnoticeable nuance to our story makes it all extremely real, and one of the very reasons why I love the Bible.

A bleeding woman comes up behind Jesus to touch the edge of His cloak. This is another desperate person. Because of her medical condition, she has been neglected and ostracized by many. Jewish laws concerning blood and diseases keep her husband from having sex with her or even doing life together. She can't have any kids. If she already had kids, they would have forgotten what Mom looked like. Domestically this poor soul can't hang out with people she's called friends for the past twelve years. Jewish law declares anyone who touches this bleeding woman to be unclean. If this woman sits down, the chair she sits in is deemed unclean. For twelve long years she has been isolated and lonely. She is not allowed to go to the community center or to the temple. Corporate worship is taken away from her. Physically she feels weak and unable to cope. Emotionally this nameless female is a wreck. This is a fragile, marginalized, depressed woman with a decimated self-image. With great courage and disguise, she manages a maneuver to touch Jesus. With one touch her bleeding stops.

I've met many women who are lonely, isolated, and not connected. Most never thought they would end up as such. These same women are driven to other women, female community groups, or an organization like MOPS (Mothers Of Pre Schoolers) exactly because of their desperation. Will your desperation cause you to brave a touch of Jesus?

Luke chapter eight portrays two very desperate people who are white-knuckled and anxious for a demonstration of God's power. The desperation factor drives Jairus and an anonymous woman to seek the very source of power. If you need a display of power, can you gauge your level of desperate motivation? Are you as desperate for Jesus as you are for oxygen or water... or Starbucks latte?

Before kids, Sherry and I found ourselves on the beach in sunny South Carolina. It was July, and we were being baked in a 100+ degree frying pan. We tried walking to the next visible pier as a creative way to tan. Our tanning turned into dehydrated desperation. A personified ocean began mocking our thirst. The irony of salty water became a living metaphor of our own desperation. I had to find something to drink, or my young marriage might quickly be in jeopardy.

Like a wonderful mirage, a frozen lemonade cart began peering through the heat waves about a quarter mile down the beach. For a trifling $2.50 this mirage could become a refreshing reality for my bride and me. Between the two of us, we had our swimsuits and 43 cents. Sherry's eyes urgently communicated, "You either figure out how to buy a frozen lemonade, or figure out how you're going to cart me to the hospital!" I made my way to the frozen lemonade guy. With all the boldness a skinny, burnt pastor can muster, I asked for 43 cents worth of frozen lemonade. He obliged, and we survived. Frozen lemonade has never tasted so good.

How desperate are you? The cable news networks have story after story of desperation. During down trends and recessions, some people will burn down their homes when facing foreclosure. That's desperation. When banks move in to take homes, some families decide nobody will have their house, including themselves. Ironically, after jail time, these human portraits of desperation will still have to pay for the house they burnt down. That is total desperation.

God's power seems to flow in times of desperation. This spiritual equation may be somewhat difficult to see unfold in America. However, you can certainly see the connect between God and desperation in places like Peru and Kenya. In these third world countries, people make their residents in city dumps. The poorest of the poor don't have the luxury of soup kitchens to know where their next meal will come from. Desperate people are crying out for God to move, and God is doing supernatural things.

My friend, Carl, was a missionary in Lebanon for 13 years. Over breakfast, Carl speaks often of the Lebanese people who are war torn and desperate. Carl has heard these distressed people cry out to Jesus. Carl will also blow you away with stories of miracles, power, and people being raised from the dead. Immediately my American faith begins to hesitate when Carl starts his crazy story telling. But Carl is a solid, non-sensationalist, reasonable, and credible friend. There's really no good reason to doubt what Carl tells me, and so I don't. When we're desperate enough to cry out loud to Jesus, surrender, and fall at His feet… no matter what anybody might say… power starts to flow.

Could it be that Jesus is actually looking for people to give power to? A distressed woman touches Him, and it stops Jesus dead in His claustrophobic tracks. Remember, there are two stories going on at one time. As this woman's bleeding stops, Jairus is waiting on Jesus, and getting more anxious as time is seemingly slipping by. Jesus stops and asks His friends who touched Him. As if Peyton Manning would call time out and ask a stadium full of Colts, er… Bronco fans who yelled his name, Jesus wants to know who touched him. Hordes of people are choking, suffocating, crowding, and Jesus wants to know what ONE person touched him. Are you kidding me? Jesus checks His power gauge, and there has been a withdrawal. He wants to know who is on the receiving end. Jesus has available power, and apparently it can be transferred into people. Amazing.

The bleeding woman can sense her cover is about to be blown. Jesus seems to be really upset. The ensuing scenario might possibly be a riot or stampede of Biblical proportions. Literally hundreds would have been deemed unclean with proximity to such an indiscriminate person. A scared, desperate woman comes clean and falls at Jesus's feet. It's curious how exchanges of Jesus's power seem to often coincide with desperately falling at His feet.

Why does Jesus go off about someone touching Him? Everyone is pushing and shoving and trying to get close. Isn't this an unreasonable request to know the ONE who touched Him? However, a detailed Dr. Luke includes how this bleeding woman touches the edge of Jesus' cloak. The Greek word for "edge" actually means tassel. Jewish people are known to have garments with tassels. This follows an Old Testament ordinance where people would sew tassels onto clothes to remember Torah. Some tassels or tzitzits have five knots tied. Each knot helps them remember Torah... Genesis, Exodus, Leviticus, Numbers, Deuteronomy. Each knot is cause to rehearse entire books of scripture committed to memory since early teenage years. (Doesn't this make my memorized badge of John 3:16 seem so lame?)

Tassels are also sewn onto the ends of prayer shawls. If you cover your head with a prayer shawl, Jewish rabbis say you are going into your prayer closet. Jewish prayer shawls are also called wings. With a prayer shawl placed on your shoulders and arms, the spread of an eagle's wings is colorfully animated. A prayer shawl is considered the wings of a rabbi. Late in the Old Testament, approximately 400 years before Jesus was born, a prophecy was recorded about the Messiah and His wings. "But for you who revere my name the Son of righteousness will rise with healing in its wings." (Malachi 4:2) These are prophetic words about Jesus. He would come with healing in His wings... in His prayer shawl with the tassels sewn to the hem.

The bleeding woman does all she could to touch the edge or hem of Jesus' clothes. Does she touch His prayer shawl... His tassels...His wings? Does this woman know her Old Testament prophecy like her own toothbrush? Does she know Jesus is the Messiah who comes with healing in His wings? Maybe that's why she so desperately wants to touch the hem of His garment.

No wonder Jesus wants to know who touched Him. No wonder He's asking what seemed to be a ridiculous question. He wants to meet the person who believes He is the Messiah. He wants to meet the person who knows their Bible, and believes there will be healing in His hand-sewn wings. Jesus is looking for such hungry people to dole out power to.

God is still looking for people to give power to. He is surfing global social networks looking for desperate hearts fully committed to Him and His Word. (II Chronicles 16:9) Don't box God into a stingy corner. If you're having power problems, the electrical short is on your end. Can there be a delay in God's power even for desperately seeking Christians? Power is available, but delays are also inevitable.

Jesus looks at the woman who has been powerfully delivered from 12 painful years of bleeding and says, "daughter…" It's an endearing word for the woman who believes in Jesus's wings, but a maddening term for a Mr. Jairus who has been on stand by for far too long. He has endured the delay, but what about *his* daughter? Is she still alive? Just when Jesus dubs the healed bleeding woman as His adopted daughter, someone pushes through the crowd and announces Jairus' daughter has died.

Rulers of synagogues like Jairus gave commands and people followed orders. Jesus had been asked, not commanded, to heal Jairus' dying daughter. The bleeding woman wasn't dying. Her condition had been endured for 12 years. What would a few more hours have mattered? If Jesus had only prioritized the medical diagnosis, perhaps Jairus' daughter would not be dead. Jesus's delay did not make much sense to Jairus nor us.

Like me, I'm assuming you struggle with God's timing. An unplanned expense, threatening health issues, pangs of divorce, devastating addictions of someone close, resumes eliciting no responses, a need for clarity of purpose... all pit us against God's timing and ours. You've prayed those consistent, constant, desperate prayers over and over. One more pat on the shoulder from another Christian saying, "Don't stop believing," and you're going to be pushed over the edge. What do you do when there's a delay in His power?

In a very dramatic moment, Jesus tells a disorientated father, "Don't be afraid; just believe, and she will be healed." There it is... again. Just believe. Just believe. The delay in power has caused his daughter's death, and Jesus says, "Just believe." It borders on the ridiculous. It feels like the calm of Jesus is in direct opposition to the debilitating grief of a dad. This feels more like a complete power failure rather than delay.

Jairus leads Jesus through the maze of people and his own angst. They arrive at his house. Outside, professional, paid mourners have already begun their paid ritual of wailing and crying. Jesus commands the lament to stop because, as He claims, the daughter is only sleeping. Mourning quickly turns to laughter because these insincere people know dead when they see it.

Was this little girl really dead? Skeptics trying to remove the miraculous from miracles would agree with Jesus. Jairus' daughter was, in fact, only sick and asleep. Inserting some historical, cultural context into our power story would be helpful at this point. In ancient Palestine, bodies decomposed very fast because of a harsh, dry, hot climate. When a person died, mourners often arrived within the hour to assure the burial would be hurried along. A dead, smelly body did nobody any good. This is why Jairus' mourners were poking fun at Jesus's suggestion. They know dead. They definitely know the *smell* of dead!

DOCTOR Luke writes about this young girl's spirit returning. This is a meticulous doctor's way of initialing and then cancelling the death certificate. Jesus brings life to another daughter, and immediately asks for someone to give her something to eat. I love how Jesus has the power, authority, and compassion to cover both big and small needs.

How will we handle our power problems and God's potential delay? In times of desperation when God seems silent, that's when we'll discover the depth and authenticity of our faith. While praying and crying through God's power delays, that's when we begin to see our faith as either real or plastic. From God's perspective, when *is* our faith real? Does God see our faith as real when we cry out or when we have to endure a delay? Does crying determine faith, or does waiting without shaking a fist at God?

Paul Potts's dream was to sing. Singing was all Paul wanted to do, but this basset hound-faced, pudgy, crooked teeth, dreamer didn't fit a pop star mold. Potts spent all of his discretionary income on singing lessons. His constant prayer was simply, "God, I just want to sing, I just want to sing, I just want to sing." At age 36, Paul Potts had no gigs and was in desperate need for power. The delay in his dreams and prayers had all but crushed him.

He worked in a car phone warehouse. Paul was on the brink of poverty while suffering through appendicitis, a broken collarbone, and a benign tumor. With his last few pence, one last singing lesson was taken, and an audition for Britain's Got Talent show was secured.

There had been a thirty-six year power delay. In 2007 the switch went on. Paul Potts stepped up to the mic to sing for the judge's panel (including American Idol's Simon Cowell). Paul belted out the operatic Giacomo Puccini's "*Nessun dorma*". Paul received a standing ovation from the audience of 2,000 people, and the rest is music history. Check out the Youtube video and join the applause.

The greater the delay, the greater the demonstration of power. The more God delays, the more demonstration of power will happen. The greater the delay, the greater the miracle. What was true for a bleeding woman, Jairus, and Paul Potts, can be true for you.

Somebody will invariably respond to this play for power and ask: What if you pray for somebody who is really sick and they die? You've prayed for power, but they kick the bucket without finishing their bucket list. How do you deal with this power delay, Pastoooor? (these "take that" gems are primarily used to pin pastors to necessarily padded church world walls...)

The greater the delay, the greater the demonstration of power. For someone who dies but followed Jesus, there's a greater demonstration of power that will take place someday. The greater the delay, the greater the demonstration of power. Christians who follow Jesus will experience death, burial, and a resurrection in the same way Jesus did. This is a real, physical resurrection where body meets up with soul once again. THAT is a great demonstration of power. Resurrection is a greater demonstration of power. A lesser form of power is when a sick person gets healed. Eventually they will still die. Someone who dies and is brought back to life is the greater display of power.

God's power is resurrection power, and it takes us beyond life itself. You do want some of this, don't you? Why would anyone settle for anything less? Why would anyone not grab onto Jesus's complete healing power.

When Jesus told the bleeding woman her faith had "healed" her, and when he told Jairus his daughter would be "healed" --- Jesus used the Greek word "sozo." This rich word goes far beyond the confines of a physical healing. Sozo also includes delivering someone from evil. Sozo is a spiritual rescuing. Sozo is a reconciling of a lost person back to God. Sozo is salvation. Sozo is restoration of peace and shalom.

Salvation is what God's resurrection power really looks like. Eternal life now and later encapsulates Jesus's powerful use of sozo.

God's power is not just for your finances, it's also to save somebody. God's power is not just for your marriage, it's for salvation. That's what God's power looks like. When God's power comes into your broken marriage, it is to bring two people together to be saved and restored by God. When God's power comes over your addiction, it's not just for your addiction; it's so you will be saved. When power comes into your work place, it's not just to give you a better job; it's because somebody there needs sozo. It might even be you.

That's what God's power looks like. What is forcing you to settle for anything less? Stop, drop, and pray right now. Ask God to show His power to you. He's looking for desperate people who still believe there's sozo in His wings. God does not have a power problem even if you feel terminally corroded as a Christian. Desperate, surrendered Jesus followers are welcome swimmers in the river of Jesus's unmatched flow of power. There's still healing and power in His wings. I dare you to touch. I dare you to ask.

Chapter End Notes

1. Jerusalem Vacation, http://jokes4all.net/joke_2431.html
2. ThinkExist.com Quotations. "Maureen Dowd quotes".
ThinkExist.com Quotations Online 1 Mar. 2012. 5 Apr. 2012
http://en.thinkexist.com/quotes/maureen_dowd/
3. Jim Cymbala, Fresh Power; (Grand Rapid, MI; Zondervan
2001) pg. 26-27.
4. Mark Driscoll, Confessions of a Reformission Rev; (Grand
Rapids, MI;   Zondervan 2006) pg. 91.

Chapter Nine

Drop In The Bucket

Strategy #9: Decide to serve and help.

Luke 9:10-17

"When the apostles returned, they reported to Jesus what they had done. Then he took them with him and they withdrew by themselves to a town called Bethsaida, but the crowds learned about it and followed him. He welcomed them and spoke to them about the kingdom of God, and healed those who needed healing. Late in the afternoon the Twelve came to him and said, "Send the crowd away so they can go to the surrounding villages and countryside and find food and lodging, because we are in a remote place here." He replied, "You give them something to eat." They answered, "We have only five loaves of bread and two fish—unless we go and buy food for all this crowd." (About five thousand men were there.) But he said to his disciples, "Have them sit down in groups of about fifty each." The disciples did so, and everybody sat down. Taking the five loaves and the two fish and looking up to heaven, he gave thanks and broke them. Then he gave them to the disciples to set before the people. They all ate and were satisfied, and the disciples picked up twelve basketfuls of broken pieces that were left over."

A pastor stood up and walked to the pulpit at the front of his overtly liturgical church. Each week the pastor would throw out an automatic, "And the Lord be with you." The congregation would respond with a memorized, "And also with you." Over the years, this exchange of liturgy had lost some of zip and meaning. Without much thought, church goers would let their, "And also with you," fly. One memorable Sunday the pastor manned his station and mouthed words, which nobody could hear. There was a technical glitch with his microphone. After switching to a more capable mic, the first audible sounds out of the pastor's mouth were, "There was a problem with the microphone." The immediate congregation's rote response was, "And also with you!"

At times I try to gauge if there is a problem with the pastor at our church... and I BE the pastor! If there is a pastor problem, talking about serving can just make things harder. Challenging crowds to get going can either fire up people or get the pastor fired. Weird how that can work. I like to talk a lot about serving outside the church walls. Authentic Christians must live beyond the confines of an hour or so on Sunday morning. A few years back, someone coined the phrase, "Stop going to church and start being the Church." Although this little axiom, for some, has turned into yet another Christian cliché, it still resonates within seriously hungry people who want to change the world.

If you could see me with a basketball in my hands, you would say I look goofy. Even if I try to act like I know what I am doing, you would still say... "goofy." Put that same basketball in the hands of LeBron James, and suddenly you're putting the Miami

Heat in contention for another NBA championship. It really does depend on whose hands things are in. A golf ball in my hands looks as natural as a moon rock. In the hands of Tiger Woods, it looks like a multi-million dollar Nike contract regardless of life off the links. It just depends on whose hands that tiny white ball is in. Drum sticks or an artist's paint brush have no redeeming value in my paws. Any art form I may try to mimic will be ugly. A hammer placed in my possession usually results in someone getting hurt. Place these same kinds of targeted instruments into the hands of professionals and art takes flight. Homes are built. A gun in the wrong hands creates terroristic fear. That same gun, placed into the trained hands of a police officer, will gain security and freedom. A gun placed in to the hands of a skilled hunter puts tender, juicy venison on the dinner table. It all depends on whose hands it's in.

What's in your hands, and how will you use your something to help? How will you serve and make a world-changing impact --- regardless of what the pastor does or does not do.

The popular story of Jesus feeding 5,000 men (there were probably four times that number if you include women and children) with a couple breadsticks and five fish filets is found in all four Gospel books. God is sending a loud signal that He wants us to get something from this story. He hasn't repeated the same story four times just to destroy more of His spectacular rain forest. There is something here to get through our thick, religious skulls. This grand story repeated in Matthew, Mark, Luke, and John have different and wonderful details specific to each writer. If you have ears to hear, you can't help but understand this most beloved flannel graph story. It's obviously a favorite of God's as well.

You've probably discovered this truth to be true: Helping people almost always comes at inopportune times. You've noticed this, right? Serving, helping, and meeting people's needs usually happens in time slots you've doggedly reserved for leisure. Why is this?

Jesus's disciples have just returned from being sent out to minister in power. These Apostles were commissioned to preach, heal, and cast out demons. These are the well-known twelve talmidim of Rabbi Yeshua. These are Jesus's hand-selected church staff, and they are all coming back home from an awesome missions trip. At the same time, Jesus hears the staggering news of His cousin John's ruthless beheading. What dynamics are in play as Jesus and His close friends meet back up? The disciples are emotionally and physically drained, but also spiritually energized. Jesus is reeling emotionally from the loss of a close family member. A smart decision is made to catch up and grab some long overdue R&R. A place across the lake from Capernaum would be the perfect refuge for a team retreat. This remote getaway is nestled in the quiet village of Bethsaida. Only about 3,000 people lived there, and most of the locals were known to keep quietly to themselves. Nobody would bother this tired gang of spiritual giants in Bethsaida. For this retreat, each anxious participant would throw together a basket of staples including a bottle of wine and some Pop-Tarts (or something like that). They would eat, relax, and be rejuvenated with the tight bond of good friends.

Someone in the press leaks news of this retreat weekend. Crowds not only hear about the retreat, but follow like annoying paparazzi. If you were one of the disciples, you're feeling invaded and violated about now. You're also feeling some aggravation as Jesus welcomes the burgeoning throngs of humanity with open arms. Close friends are looking forward to some chill, secluded time with Jesus and a glass of Bordeaux. Jesus, on the other hand, seems to encourage the interruption. Jesus starts helping and talking to the frenzied people about the Kingdom. Can't you see the eyes of the disciples start to roll as their time to breathe is getting cut short before it even starts? Serving and helping people seems to always come at the most inopportune time.

Each summer I take a contracted study break to enjoy my own time of rejuvenation. A favorite refuge for these special times is Myrtle Beach, South Carolina. My study break is a sacred, annual time that has been prioritized and revered for years. Once a year, beach front property is turned into holy ground, and my approach is always of utmost seriousness. It's my necessary time away (with family) to read, pray, worship, write and get recharged for another year.

A few summers ago, I was lapping up the sun and a smoothie at Myrtle Beach. Alone with my Bible and a glorious sunrise, I was reading and feeling God's smile. Suddenly an abrupt lady made a beeline to my beach chair and said, "I happened to notice that you were reading your Bible. Are you a Christian?" "Well … as a matter of fact, I'm a pastor," I replied. "Really! You're a PASTOR?" With that, a complete and shoeless stranger let it all hang out. Usually people like car salesmen or bartenders run when they find out I'm a pastor --- especially after they've just dropped an endearing "F" bomb. This woman was excited to get free beach side counseling. She went on and on about the devastation of her recent divorce. "Blah, blah, blah. Yadda, Yadda, Yadda," was all I heard. Inside I was thinking an almost prayer. "Lord, I'm trying to worship You. I'm trying to rest in Your awesome and sunny presence, but this woman is a distraction. She is a nuisance, Lord. Please remove her from the face of the earth."

Why is it that, more often than not, helping and serving people comes at the most inopportune times? I've never met a dead person who died at a convenient time. Every time somebody dies and I'm asked to do the funeral, it's always the most inconvenient time. Nobody has learned how to die at a good time! What's up with THAT?

Most annoyingly often, genuine service unfolds at weird, hard times. That is a universal truth, and Jesus is universally trying to teach us something. It can take a lifetime to learn, but when you walk in the presence of Jesus, personal agendas tend to get erased. Serving means welcoming as Jesus welcomed, even when our own needs are pressing in.

As Jesus teaches and helps and serves, the sun begins to set. His friends come to Him and request all the people be sent away so the masses can hit the local restaurants and motels. Jesus tells His disciples they should provide dinner. You gotta love the chutzpah of Jesus!

The Bible writer John gives us the well-known information about a little boy with a sack lunch containing five loaves of bread and two fish. That is all the food Jesus's staff could get their hands on. They can go into town and buy some food, but ten to twenty thousand people will most definitely bust the love-offering bank. What about the food each of the disciples had packed? Didn't they each pack some wine and Pop-Tarts? Can't they use their own food?

The Bible writer Mark tells us that Jesus's friends are so busy with this crowd of people, the disciples don't get a chance to eat (Mark 6:31). It's an interesting detail, but begs the question: Where are they hiding their own stash of food? Maybe they had managed to break open their picnic baskets during one of Jesus's lectures, and now their own grub is gone. But what if (and let's be overly cynical) they actually lied about their own food and only offer a measly lunch from a school kid? That is appalling. If this is true, their license to be an Apostle should be hurriedly revoked.

If God calls me to take a short-term mission trip to Haiti, and I say, "I don't have the money to do that," am I as guilty as the deceptive disciples? Isn't that appalling too? What if I argue that I just don't have the money --- but I do have cable TV, newly released DVD's, and a daily brew of Starbucks? Does that make me a tainted disciple too? Will you ever withhold your resources if God compels you to serve?

What on earth will God do if we withhold our
resources? Will His sovereign plan be thwarted by our
tightfistedness? If we don't put our resources back
into His hands, God will find another venue to help
and serve the people He loves. His purposes will not
be foiled by our stinginess.

Let's be a little more optimistic and suggest the
Apostles don't have any food. At the very least,
maybe they already ate their own food. All they really
have now is a boy's packed lunch. That's what is
available to try and feed the hungry crowd. If this is
true, then anytime God calls us to serve --- in whatever
extreme circumstance --- He will give us the means to
do so. Does Jesus really expect His ragtag team of
twelve to feed 20,000 people? Seriously? What He
expects of them is to take whatever they have and to
place it into His hands. Remember, it all depends on
whose hands it's in.

When you venture to developing countries like
Kenya, you'll be blown away by the absolute poverty.
Starving kids, hopeless adults, and people living in 10'
x 10' shacks will haunt you. Faced with extreme need,
most of us tend to get the "drop in the bucket"
mentality. It's easy to turn away from impossible need
after deciding anything you attempt will only be a drop
in the bucket.

Herbert and Ruth Ngunyi live in Kiserian,
Kenya. It could be easy for the Ngunyis to be
overwhelmed by the desperate need they see every
day. Instead of the "drop in the bucket" mindset,
Herbert and Ruth look at what is already in their
hands. Tea and bread. Ruth takes what is in her hands

and puts it in the hands of Jesus. Every weekend, somehow hundreds of starving Kenyan kids get tea and bread, and God has supernaturally enabled Ruth to continue this labor of love. Does Jesus expect the Ngunyis to feed all the kids by themselves, or simply place what they have into His hands? Herbert and Ruth would love to give the kids one good meal a week. Beyond tea and bread, they want to feed the kids rice and porridge one day a week. Once again the Ngunyis will take what's in their hands and put it in the hands of Jesus. It all depends on whose hands it's in.

Each time people from our church take off from Hartsfield-Atlanta airport on a grand missions trip, I know they will be harshly confronted with staggering need. I always hope they don't try to meet those needs by themselves. I really don't think that's what Jesus is expecting. Rather, it's what He can do with what they place in His competent hands. I trust you see the difference.

Less than a quarter mile down from our church's gathering place is an elementary school called Argyle. This place of hope serves the poor and diverse of Cobb County, Georgia. Directly across the street from Argyle is a massive apartment complex called home for single moms, illegal immigrants, and people barely making it. There are huge needs among the white, black, and Hispanic population. It's so easy for folks living in the "burbs" to drive by these desperate sights with something whispered about "a drop in the bucket." Anything tried won't make a dent, much less a sustained difference.

Maria Lee said, "I'm going to take whatever's in my hands, and put it in the hands of Jesus." Maria's son, Johanne, had school friends who lived in the Argyle districted apartment complex. Maria started bringing one of her son's friends to church. One friend quickly turned into a crammed car load of smiling Hispanics. That handful of kids has mushroomed to 40+ and an after-school mentoring program called Echo. This ministry has become so successful that local gangs are feeling threatened by their loss of influence to Echo. Initially, Maria didn't know what to do with the mountainous need in her own back yard. All she could do was to take what was in her hands and put it into the hands of Jesus so He could do the spectacular.

Cumberland Community Church, the church I get to pastor, sits strategically in the middle of Smyrna, Georgia, the Argyle school district, and stomping grounds of Echo kids. Hundreds of thousands live within a tight radius of the church. The church facility is 88,000 square feet, and home to a growing number of Christians. Jesus followers. Good things have happened at CCC, but leadership has struggled with greatness. The surrounding needs have reached levels of greatness, and so the church cannot settle for good. Sometimes the circumstances seem daunting, and the "drop in the bucket" attitude can short circuit well-meaning brainstorming sessions. Jesus is not asking Cumberland to figure it all out. He's whispering, "Cumberland, what do you have, and will you place it in My hands?" God is able to do more than we can begin to ask or imagine ---

according to His power and what we put in His hands. (Ephesians 3:20)

When Jesus puts a young Jewish kid's lunch into His hands, who is the consequent miracle for? Is it for the hungry or the interrupted needing some R&R?

Jesus takes a kid's happy meal and gives thanks. He lifts the food and His eyes upward. He prays out loud. He prays with His eyes open. Try that one at the next Thanksgiving gathering. Does Jesus say, "Bless this food, Lord?" The traditional Jewish prayer before a meal would read: "Praise be to You, Adonai our God, King of the universe, who brings forth bread from the earth." Most of the time we pray, "Bless this food." Rabbi Jesus would bless God as a dinner time prayer. Try that one around the Thanksgiving table. If you have food to eat, your food is already blessed. Try blessing and thanking and worshipping God instead. That will be praying like Jesus!

Jesus's friends take the food and begin passing it out and then promptly collecting the leftovers. Leftovers? Yep, they clean up and gather 12 baskets full of leftovers. This is after 5,000 men politely burp to give their satisfied approval. Imagine that scene! Twelve baskets were brimming with the accumulation of God's leftovers. Wait a minute --- where did they get the twelve baskets? How did these suddenly show up?

Maybe they are the Apostles' baskets. Remember the wine and Pop-Tarts the disciples packed for a much-anticipated getaway with their favorite rabbi? Those baskets are now loaded. They have enough food, even after thousands have been fed, to give them hang time with Jesus for a few more days of restoration. They now have enough food to have a great retreat with Jesus.

Here's another universal truth stemming from serving. When you decide to serve and help (even though it's a pain in the rear sometimes), God takes really good care of you as well.

There are still a few people scattered among us (labeled Christians) who believe they're quoting scripture when they tell a heathen friend, "God helps those who help themselves." Problem is, you can't find that much-loved verse in the BIBLE! What the Bible does promote is how God helps those who help others. God helps and grows and stretches and deepens and protects those who serve.

Jesus challenges His friends to feed and serve others because He is about to pass the Kingdom torch. The miracle performed is for the disciples and not necessarily just for the thousands needing dinner. The miracle Jesus unfolds is to further the dependency of the Apostles on Him. They need to learn what Jesus can do with whatever is in their hands. Learning this kind of eternal stuff can't happen in a classroom. Jesus puts His friends and disciples into real life, inconvenient, crisis situations where faith in God's handling of matters becomes what matters. Why do you think your neighbor is sitting on your couch in tears? Why would a co-worker unload the crumbling details of his marriage in the strange borders of your cubicle? Perhaps God is growing you through serving them. What's in your hands that God can use to impact a life? If you open up your hands in the middle of these serving interruptions, I bet you'd find a God who is quick to take care of you as well.

A flat tire in downtown Atlanta can often be the impetus for unforgettable adventure. A deflated tire afforded my friend, Jane, a full dose of story, challenge, and teaching. Meandering towards Jane's disabled vehicle, a homeless couple stopped and asked to help. The woman was very pregnant, and the man outgoing and capable. Jane found out the couple weren't married but hoped to be soon. With the last lug nut tightened, Jane invited her new homeless friends to church. They showed up the very next Sunday. They had a great time worshipping and seeing Jane again. Somewhere in the thick of this unlikely friendship, Jane felt God tapping her on the shoulder and inquiring, "Would you let them move in with you? Would you invite them into your house?" Jane had seen their inner-city cardboard box home. The address was conveniently located under an overhead bridge. Jane made comparisons of her home and theirs, and sensed God's prompting was more than an emotional nudge. Jane didn't live in a castle, but in her hands was a house with plenty of spare room. Although she was a young, single woman who needed to think through issues of expectations and safety, Jane decided to invite them to stay under her roof. So she drove back downtown to find her new friends. Once found, the homeless couple beamed at Jane because they had a gift for her. They couldn't wait to see Jane again to give her a brand new sweater "still in the wrapper." Jane is usually not at a loss for words, but this urban scenario had her stunned. They had a gift for her? This awkward exchange segued nicely to Jane's God-driven invitation. As the first nervous syllable was about to slip out, the young pregnant woman blurted, "Jane, by the way --- God gave us a new place to live! We've moved into a great shelter! Thanks for helping us." Was all of this for the homeless couple or was God doing a deepening through Jane's willingness to serve? Probably both.

Who will you serve by giving God what you're holding? What stories are waiting for you to jump into? God will help those who help others. The greatest, we're promised, are the ones who are servers and helpers. You can't call yourself a Christian if you refuse to serve like Christ. If you've bought this book, that's a fair indication you have resources to help. You have some thing (s) in your hands. Many hold their things with closed, tight fists. It's hard to lift open hands to Jesus in worship when we're clenching our stuff. That same stuff placed in the hands of Jesus will blow hurting people and you away. Having done this, you'll be amazed at how much more your open hands can grab onto Jesus in worship. And... those drops in God's bucket really begin to add up and overflow into His glorious Kingdom where Jesus followers... Christians... really do make a huge difference.

Chapter Ten

Smells Like A King

Strategy #10: Smell like Jesus.

Luke 9:18-22

"Once when Jesus was praying in private and his disciples were with him, he asked them, "Who do the crowds say I am?" They replied, "Some say John the Baptist; others say Elijah; and still others, that one of the prophets of long ago has come back to life."
"But what about you?" he asked. "Who do you say I am?" Peter answered, "God's Messiah." Jesus strictly warned them not to tell this to anyone. And he said, "The Son of Man must suffer many things and be rejected by the elders, the chief priests and the teachers of the law, and he must be killed and on the third day be raised to life."

John Ortberg once kicked off a main session of a Willow Creek church conference by asking an incredibly loaded question. Ortberg explained how an informal survey was taken with conference attendees as they entered the doors. The question was simple. How many churches are represented today? There were many different kinds of church backgrounds sitting under one conference roof. A count of Methodists, Presbyterians, Baptists, and 28 other of our 31 flavors were to be considered in this exercise. Ortberg asked the murmuring audience to turn to the person sitting next to them and make an audible guess of the elusive number. How many churches were being touted at this conference? There was an electric buzz as if a new, cheesy Christian T-shirt was hanging in the balance with the right answer. Ortberg silenced the crowd as he walked to a blank, white board and wrote the answer. 1.

The Bible says there is only one Church. This Church has one faith. One baptism. God's Church has one Lord. (Ephesians 4:5) His name is Jesus. How do you define Him? Go ahead and take a break to think about it. Do a Google search on Jesus. Some 504 million search results will pop up quickly. What are others saying about Jesus? Scan the many images. What have we made Jesus to look like? There's a manly Jesus, a hippie Jesus, a blonde-haired-blue-eyed American Jesus, a whimpy Jesus, and a WWF Jesus.

When I bury freshly redeemed souls through baptism, I ask for a powerful phrase to be repeated. With a military cadence we resolve: "I believe that Jesus is the Christ, the Son of God. I confess Him as my Lord, my Savior, and my Master." (Romans 10:9) What are the ramifications of saying and believing a creed like that? It's a clear creed signifying what we believe about Jesus. What should life look like after making such a bold declaration?

In the book of Luke, Jesus is seen doing spectacularly cool things. He heals people. Jesus raises decomposing folks from the dead. He calms an erupting earthquake, and feeds 20,000 with a Happy Meal. After building an impressive resume' of shock and awe, Jesus asks His friends (and us), what they think? He wants to know how the populace in general defined Him. What are people saying?

I do this kind of thing during elections. I want to know what Fox, CBS, NBC, ABC, CNN, and my co-workers think about emerging candidates vying for election landslides in the primaries. I want to know what the pundits, broadcasters, radio talk-show hosts, and polls say about these potential political leaders. I like to eavesdrop on political conversations at Starbucks. Usually I do this with my ear buds in to really be subversive in my savvy eavesdropping.

What was being said about Jesus in the ancient coffee shops? Talk on the street pitted Jesus as a reincarnation of John the Baptist, Elijah, or maybe one of the iconic Old Testament prophets. Those actually weren't bad answers. Polls were attributing great power and authority to Jesus. John the Baptist had already been beheaded, so throwing his name out as your barbershop opinion would mean you were promoting resurrection power. If a bartender spouted Jesus was Elijah, bar stools would have went a spinnin' because Elijah left the earth with a chariot of fire. Would he come back any differently? If Jesus were one of those Old Testament prophets brought back to life, then power, authority, and some hell fire preaching would be attached. These were all really good, significant thoughts about Jesus. Is it possible to have really good thoughts about Jesus, but not necessarily right ones?

Can Oprah Winfrey or Rush Limbaugh have good thoughts about Jesus but not necessarily the right ones? Can the religion of Islam have very good thoughts about Jesus, but not necessarily the right ones? Many Christians have really good, warm & fuzzy thoughts about Jesus, but often aren't the right ones.

The ancient Jewish people believed that when the Messiah came, He would be a second Moses. Moses was the big dog of Judaism. Moses delivered Torah. (I love saying, "Torah!" like an old Japanese war movie.) Jewish people absolutely love Torah. Genesis, Exodus, Leviticus, Numbers, and Deuteronomy were joyously celebrated books comprising Torah. Moses was loved and revered because he hand delivered Torah. Moses was also God's man to deliver the Israelites from Egyptian slavery. As pedestals go, Moses was put on a tall one. When the anticipated Messiah came, the Jewish people believed He would be a Moses look-a-like.

A problem, however, stemmed from two distinctively different, Old Testament perspectives on a second Moses. Some felt the Messiah would come with great power. A savior with military muscle and political punch would enable God's people to be freed from any nationalistic slavery. There was a second viewpoint, which painted the Messiah as a peaceful shepherd. Love, forgiveness, and a few hippie beads would characterize this softer version of the Messiah. Which perspective was right? The Old Testament promoted both power and love being chief components of the world's Savior.

When Jesus finally hit the scene, the Jewish leaders rejected His claim to be the expected Messiah. Why? He came in love and peace like a gentle shepherd. That wasn't the kind of Messiah the Jewish Pharisees were fixated on. The nation of Israel was under the ruling thumb of Rome. Jewish leaders propagated the ancient perspective of a militaristic Messiah. They wanted some old-school wrath thrown down on the Romans. Jesus didn't seem to fill the shoes of the four-star general hoped for.

While the Jewish religious community thumbed their noses at Jesus, there were those who accepted His messianic claim. The people who openly accepted Jesus as the Christ were marginalized sinners needing love, peace, and forgiveness. Do people today still accept Jesus based on what they want and need? That Google search of Jesus will most likely be slanted towards your current circumstances. Maybe you want someone who will fix your finances, doctor's tests, or unruly kid. That's the kind of Messiah many are looking for. When this kind of thinking dominates our motivations, it's easy for us to turn into cynical Pharisees. Rejection can be lightning quick when Jesus doesn't deliver the goods of our self-determined needs. Lack of divine help can define a lacking Messiah for some.

Take a look at how Jesus defines Himself. "I am the way, the truth, and the life, and no one comes to the Father except through me." (John 14:6) Jesus says, "I'm IT!" His statement is one of the most controversial declarations in the entire Bible. Jesus defines himself as the only door; not one of many. He's the one bridge to connect with God. If this is true, what happens with the millions of Buddhists, Hindus, and Islamic people? What about the millions of great Jewish people who believe in Jehovah God but not Jesus Christ? The Jesus solution is an extremely narrow minded one. Jesus knew that. He taught His followers about two roads. One is narrow and one is fat and wide. Jesus's path is narrow and few would be on it. The other super highway will be full of people who believe in lots of ways to God. Jesus says they will be dead wrong.

Don't we despise this kind of narrow-minded talk? Isn't this kind of language exactly why our Christian demographic is viewed as bigoted, hateful, and non-tolerant? There's a real push back these days on anything that stifles. Narrow-mindedness is for less enlightened people.

But wait… I actually want my doctors to be very narrow-minded. Their diagnosis and prescriptions need to be very precise. Narrow-minded. But we hate narrow-minded thinking, right? Can you believe that in football, a quarterback can throw a pass to an outside receiver, and if one foot is in bounds and the other out --- the pass is ruled an incompletion? The receiver has to have both feet inside the white sidelines for the pass to count. Unbelievable. Narrow-minded. What would the game of football be like without clear-cut rules? Chaos and sports anarchy would empty every stadium in the NFL.

If you rob a bank, you're going to spend time in jail. That's so narrow-minded! If you find yourself on the 80th floor of a towering inferno, you'll need to find a way out. When help arrives and one specific door is your only hope, will you waste any time asking for more options? You would want your rescuer to point the way and show you the exact door. THAT is narrow-minded. Most of us live our lives with high levels of narrow-mindedness except when it comes to Jesus. With Jesus, we've been programmed to be more tolerant of other avenues, saviors, and ways to God. Jesus is attached to eternity; not sports, not jail time, not health. Jesus is about eternity. Why would anybody settle for less than narrow-minded?

The many other ways so often tolerated by a tolerance-drunk culture become the wide road Jesus warns against. C.S. Lewis believes only three available options when it comes to accepting Jesus. He's either Lord, a liar, or a stark, raving, mad lunatic.[1] This forms Lewis's familiar Trilemma for people to wrestle with.

In *Mere Christianity*, CS Lewis wrote: "A man who is merely a man, and said the sort of things Jesus said would not be a great moral teacher. He would either be a lunatic on the level with the man who says he's a poached egg, or he would be the devil of hell. You must take your choice, either this was and is the Son of God, a mad man, or something worse. You can shut him up for a fool, or you can fall at his feet and call him Lord and God. Let us not come with any patronizing nonsense about His being a great human teacher. He has not left that open to us."[2]

Jesus inquires about public opinion polls, but then turns to His friends like a chatty movie buff in a crowded theatre and asks, "What about you? What do you guys think?" How will James, John, and Matthew answer? How will the vivacious "Sons of Thunder" view Jesus? How will a greedy tax collector see Jesus? How do I?

These friends of Jesus are also students of Rabbi Jesus. They are trying their best to be just like Jesus. Rabbis and students often banter questions back and forth to test and challenge their working knowledge of scripture. Is this what Jesus was doing with His students or talmidim? Peter steps up to the chalkboard and answers, "You are the Christ of God."

The very pregnant Greek word for "Christ" is "christos." It means "Messiah" or anointed one. In ancient Hebrew days, kings were anointed with oil --- a lot of oil. Governments wanted everyone to know who the new king was, and a liberal amount of fragrant oil did the job. A grand procession with a greased up and smelly king would be the first task before commanding the throne. This aromatic oil would set the king apart as king. The scent of the king would arrive before the actual king did. Peasants along a royal parade route would know the king was coming by the fragrance preceding him. A vivid example of such an oily, official parade can be seen in I Kings 1:38-40. What IS that smell? Smells like a king!

On one powerful occasion, Jesus strolls into a Jewish synagogue and reads from a readied scroll. Jesus verbalizes words from the Old Testament prophet, Isaiah. Curiosity about Jesus is peaking, and eyes pop as Jesus reads, "The Spirit of the Lord is on me because He has anointed me." (Isaiah 62:1) If you are Jewish and living in the first century, your mind immediately thinks about Jesus being a king. He's been anointed. He's been set apart. Was He doused with smelly bottle of massage oil? A week before Jesus is nailed to the cross, He is. Just before He sits on a donkey and parades into Jerusalem, Jesus is anointed with a lot of oil. (John 12:1-18) A woman uses an entire jar of very expensive and fragrant oil to anoint Jesus. Immediately after this malodorous scene, Jesus's friends plop Him atop a donkey and off to a parade they go. People throw down palm branches in front of Jesus as He rides into Jerusalem like royalty; like a king. Hundreds shout "Hosanna" as Jesus cruises by. Undoubtedly some Jr. High kid elbows a friend and says, "Certainly smells like a king."

In the 1st century you didn't bathe very often. A Saturday night scrub may be all you can get in a seven day stretch. For most people, and this includes Jesus, one set of clothes and one bath a week gets you by. It is highly probable for the entirety of Jesus's final week, He doesn't bathe. I'm guessing your kids would love to celebrate holy week without any soap or bath too. For His last week, the strong smell of aromatic oil gains Jesus a kingly reputation as He goes about town.

During that fateful, final week, Jesus literally turns the tables on cheating retailers setting up shop in the temple. Why doesn't anyone argue with His commerce-stopping antics? Is it because of the smell? Does His stately odor give Him instant authority?

Religious leaders like the Pharisees and high priests put Jesus through mock, early-morning trials. They keep asking Jesus if He is a king. Why? Does

He smell like one? A high-ranking Roman leader named Pilate asks Jesus about His status of king. Is it the eau de emperor cologne emanating from our Lord? Why do a group of insecure and ruthless Roman soldiers decide to put a robe and crown on Jesus? Why does their vicious mocking include utensils of a king like a crown and a scepter? Perhaps they are bothered by Jesus's scent.

All of this makes the Apostle Paul's words even more captivating. "Thanks be to God, who always leads us in triumphal procession in Christ (another parade) and through us spreads everywhere the fragrance (more oil) of the knowledge of Him. For we are to God the aroma of Christ..." (II Corinthians 2:15) Jesus is a king who smells like He's been anointed. We are to smell just like Him.

Christians should smell kingly, anointed, and just like Jesus. Statistics are screaming that most don't. Most church members smell more like those outside the Church. In terms of pornography, addictions, divorce, abuse, and money management, we tend to smell stale and selfish like those who know nothing of Jesus's unselfish Kingdom. French philosopher, Blaise Pascal, is credited by some for the concept of a God-shaped hole in all of us. This is a good concept if the divinely created hole is filled fully with the authority of Jesus and complimented with a death of our selves. Pascal's concept is made better when we realize our God-shaped hole is the size of our entire body, and not a mere tiny compartment of our heart. Donald Miller, of Blue Like Jazz fame, believes many Christians have somehow managed to fill their

God-shaped hole with just enough Jesus to get by, but without a death of self. When our God-shaped cavity is filled with a little Jesus, but the rest of our life is filled with our selfish vices, "Christian" becomes glaringly void of meaning.

Need more evidence for Jesus's rank as ruler and king? Josh McDowell created a great illustration to ease your doubts.[3] Suppose I give you a bag of 100 Susan B. Anthony silver dollars and ask you to put a permanent marker "x" on one. Placing the marked coin back with the other 99 silver pieces, I ask you to pull the "x" out blindfolded. What is the probability of finding that one coin? (Don't you hate forced math in non-math situations? This book should have come with a clearly marked math warning label. Sorry.) Your chances of finding that one Susan B. Anthony would be 1 in 100. You knew that, of course!

Let's say the state of Texas is lying gloriously in front of you and me. In a surprising twist, I have filled the entire state with Susan B. Anthony coins --- two feet deep. Crazy I know, but this is a just a weird hobby of mine. Grabbing the silver dollar with an "x" from your obvious hand-writing, we flip it into Texas and towards Amarillo. Stay with me on this. We manage to stir the entire state filled with two feet of coins. At this point I look you straight between your steely eyes and ten gallon hat, and I ask you to pull out your marked coin. What's the probability you'll find it on the first grab? It's 10 to the 17th power. This is a number requiring reams of paper to capture the amount of zeros needed.

What does this have to do with Jesus being a smelly king? In the Old Testament there are 450 specific prophesies about Jesus. At least 400 years before Jesus walked through Texas on route 66 (He didn't really do that. He took interstate 20, of course.), prophets painted amazing pictures of what His life would look like. Before Jesus came to planet Earth, there were 450 details of His birth, life, and death. Guess what the chances are for one man to precisely implement just eight of those predictions? Wish you had paid more attention in Calculus class? Mathematicians say the answer is 10 to the 17th power. That's the kind of credibility behind King Jesus. Do we live and smell like we believe the evidence?

Chris Case is an inner-city Atlanta church planter who previously worked on staff with me. Chris recently blogged, "Our theology is more about what we do than it is about what we say or believe." The best evidence for Jesus being king is an adult who volunteers their time for a summer kids' camp. Why would anyone on earth give up four nights of summer to wipe little snotty noses of strange little kids? Some adults are assigned nursery duty during summer kids' camp. Changing my own kid's diapers was hard enough, why would anyone volunteer to change someone else's? That's insane! That's the smell of Jesus! Those kingly volunteers are disposing one smell and radiating another kingly one. They are the fragrance of Jesus their King.

Why would someone take $150 hard-earned dollars and give it to an unknown Kenyan orphan so he or she can go to school? Why would people invest time to work with dreaded middle schoolers? Why would a church sacrifice a Sunday church service, so a congregational army could clean up a local high school instead? This is crazy talk! This smells like a King. This smell becomes really good evidence for lost people who don't know the smell of Jesus.

Our church has grown into a great habit of cancelling Sunday services so the body can serve our community. Because of lost offerings, we stand to lose over $100,000 annually with our intentional serving. Only by God's grace do we keep ending our fiscal year in the black as we continue being the church in such smelly ways. One particular FIA (Faith In Action) Sunday was well spent at Argyle Elementary School. Argyle is a high need/under resourced school, which serves some of the poorest in our county. After we did a massive makeover on Argyle, our church staff stopped by the school on the following Monday morning. The front office secretary greeted us immediately and beamed about the elevated attitudes of teachers and kids. Brighter and cleaner demeanors reflected the work our church had done the day before. A little 3rd grade boy talked to us and was elated about his "new" school. When we asked what he like most, this wide-eyed Hispanic boy yelled, "The bathrooms!" This young kid explained how he had never used the bathrooms at school because they were so nasty. All of that changed in the time span of one powerful Sunday. Now that was going to church! Those clean bathrooms had the wafting fragrance of Jesus.

I've smelled the smell of Jesus in marriages. There are certain people whose covenant relationship with God empowers a long-haul, covenantal marriage. These kinds of people are rare birds, and glorious aromas for other young couples to sniff out and model. Somehow and someway, fragrant marriages move beyond the seven-year itch, and refuse to let feelings override obedience. That's a scent I'd like to bottle and sell.

Unfortunately, most marriages these days don't smell too good. The lack of a sweet bouquet comes from too many husbands and wives allowing feelings to reign. The commitment of marriage these days goes only as deep as fleeting emotions. Feelings gauge paint colors at Home Depot. Marriage requires commitment. Feelings are consistently deceptive. Feelings cause affairs. Commitment creates legacy. Godly marriages have obedience as a foundation, and unconditional love as the cornerstone. When did the whole marriage world revert and depend on feelings? Jesus-smelling marriages have discovered commitment, obedience, and unconditional love result in feelings, but feelings rarely cause the opposite. Why would any marriage stick with it these days --- especially when feelings rule and fly south? Jesus really is the only answer. When I attend a 30th wedding anniversary, I can almost always detect the smell of the King.

It's a pungent smell. Take a whiff of the crazy people who proactively set aside 10% (or more) of their gross income, and then give it away with great abandonment to their church and other Kingdom efforts. Even when the economy turns downward, these smelly, hard-working believers recognize all of their resources come from their generous King. Giving a portion joyfully away keeps their aroma strong. It's nuts, right? It's evidence of Jesus. It's foolishness to confound and convict an otherwise stinky world.

My friend and co-worker, Joe Braun, has a distinct odor. Joe and his wife Jen moved from Colorado to Atlanta to work with a turn-around church --- for free. Joe had no guarantee for a sustained job and no initial pay. Why would anyone do THAT? Joe believed he was called to Atlanta --- period. He believed God would take care of the details. He was caught up in a triumphal parade, and the smell of a king was rubbing off. Seven years later, the church Joe serves is growing and employs him full-time as a key leader of community groups. King Jesus affects people like this. People like Joe are some of the best evidence of Jesus being the anointed King of Kings.

How do you define Jesus? Your answer should be independent of how your friends, cable broadcasters, or political pundits define Him. What would you say? Rabbi Jesus is looking at each one of us, and still asking the same question. "Who do YOU say I am?"

Would your answer be based on your parent's faith? If you were forced to grow up in church, your label of "Christian" may not even be yours; it could be your mom and dad's.

Once a week at the Scott house, we pull out Bibles for an interactive time of study and prayer.

Sometimes we work on memory verses. Each time we banter questions and ideas back and forth to make sure there is life application. I suggest my kids pray in ways that will force them to apply our study time. Some weeks our special time flows. Other times it drags. There are days when our get-together elicits great sighs. Often there are brilliant ideas and God-moments. Why do I push and pull my family in these God directions? I want my kids to own their faith. I want them to smell more like Jesus than me.

After Peter answers Jesus's question correctly, Jesus says something that is very hard for a disciple to hear. Jesus says it will be necessary for Him to be rejected and killed. Before glory is experienced, the Messiah will suffer. Even for Jesus's friends, this is a hard pill to swallow. This isn't the kind of Messiah they are looking for. A suffering shepherd is light-years removed from the military powerhouse they secretly hope for.

If you and I answer, "You are the Christ," following Jesus will demand our acceptance of a path that can often turn rough and hard. You OK with this? Are you ready to accept this? If you believe Jesus is King, then you need to understand how suffering, difficulties, and dying are entwined in our relationship with the Messiah.

I see more and more hurting people coming to church these days. Some are ready to give up after giving one final Sunday morning a final shot. Remember, Jesus DOES bring good news. It might be excruciating now, but glory will come. Suffering might come, but --- just as it did for Jesus --- so will glory. Are you connected to King Jesus? Can you smell Him coming? He is a king to follow. He is Lord. He's more than a good person or teacher. Jesus is anointed royalty, and He's inviting you to a grand, wonderfully aromatic parade.

Chapter End Notes

1. C.S. Lewis, <u>Mere Christianity</u>, (London, UK; Harper Collins 1952) pg. 54-56.
2. Ibid.
3. Josh McDowell, <u>Evidence That Demands A Verdict</u>; (San Bernadino, CA, Here's Life 1979) pg. 167.

alan scott

Chapter Eleven

Transfigured in a Disfigured World

Strategy #11: Live in God's presence.

Luke 9:28-36

"About eight days after Jesus said this, he took Peter, John and James with him and went up onto a mountain to pray. As he was praying, the appearance of his face changed, and his clothes became as bright as a flash of lightning. Two men, Moses and Elijah, appeared in glorious splendor, talking with Jesus. They spoke about his departure, which he was about to bring to fulfillment at Jerusalem. Peter and his companions were very sleepy, but when they became fully awake, they saw his glory and the two men standing with him. As the men were leaving Jesus, Peter said to him, "Master, it is good for us to be here. Let us put up three shelters—one for you, one for Moses and one for Elijah." (He did not know what he was saying.) While he was speaking, a cloud appeared and enveloped them, and they were afraid as they entered the cloud. A voice came from the cloud, saying, "This is my Son, whom I have chosen; listen to him." When the voice had spoken, they found that Jesus was alone. The disciples kept this to themselves, and told no one at that time what they had seen."

On average, Satan kicks people's spiritual butts eight to ten days after baptism. There are no hard facts to back up my numbers. Instead there are hard experiences. When someone decides to die to self, bury their past, and allow Jesus to take over as Lord, Satan gets testy. He wants to take back what he thought was his. Days after a momentous decision is made, Satan begins fighting back. I've seen it time and time again. A transformational decision for Jesus causes an equally dark spiritual battle. Struggle gives birth to doubt, and doubt becomes the great flame extinguisher of newbies who have taken up the banner of Christian. Approximately a week or so after huge spiritual decisions are made, there develops a real need to affirm and strengthen a newly-found faith.

The transfiguration Dr. Luke writes about was exactly eight days after Jesus's closest followers decided they were all in. The disciples made intentional decisions about Jesus. They gave Him verbal ascent and internal commitments to die and deny. Eight days later, and because of ensuing spiritual attacks, Jesus takes three of His closest friends on a proactive trip. Peter, James, and John are as dysfunctional and colorful as most of us. Peter can't keep his mouth shut, while James and John often operate as power hungry control freaks. In spite of this, Jesus knows the sincerity and depth of decisions His three companions make. Jesus is aware of the sifting Satan will attempt to do with His friends. A road trip to a mountain might just be what is needed for these followers to fight and stay the course.

Jesus begins praying. Do you wonder what this prayer time looks like? Is it on a Wednesday night like all legitimate prayer services? Does Jesus circle up His three friends, grab hands, and ask everyone to close their eyes? Did they pray clockwise? Are there prayer requests? Did anyone give one of those weird "unspoken" prayer requests? Which of the disciple's minds drift first? Who yawns and falls asleep standing up? It can happen. Jesus, Peter, James, and John climbed 9,166 feet to pray together on a mountain. Such a hike, it would seem, is not the optimal prelude to a powerful prayer time. I've grown sleepy climbing the steps of our church. You can imagine the physical reality of Jesus and His friends.

At some point, one of Jesus's friends wipes his tired eyes and gets a forbidden prayer peek at Jesus's face. Stunningly, His clothes are changing into a bleached out lightning bolt. Jesus's figure is transformed, and thus the church world term "transfiguration." Additionally, and for a touch of dramatic flare, Moses and Elijah crash the high altitude party. Moses and Elijah. These are big time dead guys showing up. They are Old Testament rock stars. A sleepy prayer time suddenly is not so much.

Peter quickly shifts from questioning the mountain retreat to fully embracing the whole occasion. The hike up the mountain has taken Peter's breath away. The prayer time has become spectacularly breath taking. Impetuously, Peter suggests tents and booths be built to house Jesus, Moses, Elijah, and Peter's own mountaintop experience. Does Peter know what he is suggesting or trying to do? Apparently not; a parenthetical statement makes Peter out as a bit of an idiot. Why does Luke write that? What is Peter doing that is so embarrassingly wrong? I would probably want to do the same, wouldn't you? Like a frozen lemonade on a hot summer's day, mountaintop experiences can give us brain freeze.

While Peter is scheming, a cloud gathers around the top of the mountain and engulfs this unusual prayer time. Any semblance of order is thrown out the window and off the mountain. God Himself joins the prayer time and speaks. Peter is thinking, "We're gonna need bigger tents!" God verbalizes His great pleasure of His singular Son. Like a gifted Father does, He holds Jesus's face and says, "You're my Son. I love you, and you're really good at what you do." With that, the cloud lifts, Moses and Elijah exit, and Jesus and His friends are left with some really goofy smiles on their faces.

So goes the transfiguration. Some believe this is one of the most magnificent events in the life of Jesus. Cool stuff, huh? Wow. Crazy. What in the world does it mean? What did it mean for Peter, James, and John? What does it mean for you and me? And you thought transfiguration was just a cool name for a Catholic church.

Biblical meaning can often be unlocked when we consider how ancient Middle Eastern Hebrew people learned truth. They did so through images, pictures, numbers, and symbols. In juxtaposition, modern day western thinkers need black and white, linear equations to find truth ($A + B = C$). However, without a grasp of creative imagery, the Bible can be a hard, if not impossible, task of interpretation (have you seen the book of Revelation?). To understand the many truths of our transfiguration story, images and symbols need to be explored. The eight days, mountain, Old Testament heroes, exodus, tents, and the cloud all entail incredibly rich imagery. These six word pictures hold truth for the taking.

One of the beginning images attached to the transfiguration is the number "8." Throughout the Bible, the number eight points to God's affirmation of His people. What happened eight days after a little Hebrew boy was born? They were circumcised to reaffirm God's covenant with the Israelites. In the great flood, how many people were saved? Eight people remained to reaffirm God's commitment and covenant to man.

How many sons did Jesse have? You guessed it, eight! Jesse's eighth son was David who became King, and God reaffirmed His plan of salvation. The Christ would come through David's family tree. Thomas saw Jesus eight days after the resurrection, and faith was reaffirmed. The Beatles sang, "Eight Days a Week," but that has nothing to do with this discussion. I just really like that song. Sorry.

Peter, James and John have a supernatural experience eight days after they make a bold stand for Jesus. Eight days symbolize a commitment, which God affirms. This transfigured getaway with Jesus affirms the commitment and faith of His three friends.

A second symbol Luke expounds on is the mountain. When we lived in Colorado, Sherry and I fell in love with the mountains. A walk outside our front door, and the Rocky Mountains begged a glorious sigh. It didn't matter what time of year or weather. Those mountains could be snow capped, summer heated, dressed in a sunrise, or bathed in a sunset --- it didn't matter. Mountains have a way of drawing you to God. It is easier to pray and worship with a grand set of mountains to soak in. I think God loves His mountains. God likes His canyons and calls them grand. He smiles at rivers and fields, but He takes tremendous pride in His mountains. Mountains are more like God. Big. Mountainous. God has a lengthy track record of telling people to go to mountains. Mountains are where people gained glimpses of the glory of God. Abraham, Moses and Elijah were told to go to a mountain. God loves mountains. Some believe God still lives in Colorado, but then how could you explain the Denver Broncos? I'm still a Colts fan. Peyton Manning is good, but he's no Rocky Top messiah.

God reveals Himself on mountains. When was the last time you had a mountaintop experience with God? I can vividly remember one of mine. In the late 90's I went to a Promise Keepers Pastors Conference. I went kicking and screaming because the promo flyer read: "Two days with 60,000 pastors in the Georgia Dome." I didn't want to spend two days with a bunch of pastors anywhere --- even in a Hawaiian dome. Pastors like to pretend everything is great and ask each other, "How many did you have Sunday?" I seriously hate that. In spite of my trepidation, I shuffled off to the Georgia Dome. There actually were 60,000 pastors there, but I met God instead. During a block of worship, He revealed Himself to me. Sixty thousand pastors were pouring their hearts out to the old hymn

"Holy, Holy, Holy." It was an amazing mountain for me. I caught a glimpse of heaven, God, and His glory. It was overwhelming; it reminded me of the heavenly creatures and angels in heaven singing, "Holy, Holy, Holy." God gave me a brief vision of His throne room written about in the book of Revelation. There was a strong lion and a slain lamb being sung to. "Holy, Holy, Holy." I was so taken aback by this experience, I had to sit down in my stadium chair and place my head in my shaking hands. I wanted to absorb the moment. I wanted to build a tent (idiot).

In that glorious moment, the pastor next to me thought I was being deeply convicted of deep, dark, secret sin. He put his hands on my head and starting praying charismatically, "Father, forgive Alan. He loves you and wants to do better, Lord." This guy just kept going and going and praying and praying. He messed up my hair, and I was having an excellent hair day. My heavenly vision quickly faded because all I could think about was punching this deluded praying pastor. My thoughts weren't so holy, holy, holy anymore.

When God grants you a special mountaintop getaway, it should change you. There's transformation when you get a glimpse of His glory. Things are different after you descend from these God moments.

Who is changed in Dr. Luke's story of the transfiguration? Jesus's face and clothes are different, but I don't think the real change happens with our Lord. The deep alterations are with Peter, James, and John. That definitive change is not something to be kept on the mountaintop. Jesus's three friends have been changed to fight the inevitable valley attacks from Satan --- approximately scheduled 8-10 days after their commitments are made. The transfiguration is more about Peter, James, and John. God changes them on the mountaintop in order to fight and to affect change with the people they will encounter living in valleys. God does the exact same thing with us today.

There's a third image or symbol to consider. Moses and Elijah represent a truck load of Hebrew/Jewish imagery. Moses was the leader who brought Torah to God's people. God's people loved Torah, and so they revered Moses. Elijah delivered God's nation from rebellion with an original display of fire on the mountain.

The Hebrew people believed the Messiah would be like Moses. Folks were also taught how Elijah would reappear just prior to the coming Messiah. Moses brought the law (Torah), and Elijah was one of the mightiest of prophets. Moses and Elijah represent the law and the prophets. When Jewish people, still to this day, refer to the Old Testament, they refer to the law and the prophets. The law and the prophets (the Old Testament) all pointed to the Messiah.

Moses and Elijah pack suitcases full of meaning for Peter, James, and John. Moses and Elijah also talk with Jesus about His departure and a fulfillment. "Fulfillment" in the Greek is a word that makes me think of Starbucks. Specifically, it brings to mind my usual Green Tea Raspberry Frappuccino. When the barista fills the cup to the brim, that's the idea of "fulfillment." When every last drop of my blended Frappuccino goes into my cup, that's fulfillment.

That's how I like it. Filled to the brim and lacking nothing. That's "fulfillment."

Moses and Elijah represent the law and the prophets. Jesus is the fulfillment of the Messiah who would come like Moses and after Elijah. In Jesus, the law and the prophets find fulfillment. Jesus fills things to the brim, and nothing is lacking. No wonder God needs a mountain for all of this.

Moses and Elijah have a conversation with Jesus about His departure. What exactly are they talking about? The word "departure" in the Greek points to the idea of an exodus. With Moses standing there, what meaning would an exodus take on? Through the leadership of Moses and God's miraculous hand, God's people were saved from Egyptian slavery. God redeemed His people. Moses was God's man to lead this mass exit or exodus. It was the whole Red Sea miracle Charlton Heston was famous for. If you don't understand that reference, you need to do your own exodus out of my generational cobwebs.

A fourth image used in the transfiguration is the tents, huts, shelters, or booths Peter wanted to build. Initially, this sounds like Peter wants to honor his honorary guests. Putting up a pup tent for Moses, Elijah, and Jesus is the least Peter can do for such distinguished guests. Why then, is Peter considered an idiot for thinking such thoughts? What is the problem there?

The idea or imagery of tents, shelters, and booths takes us back to the Jewish festival of Sukot or Feast of Tabernacles. It's also called the Feast of

Booths. Jewish people even today will set up tents or booths to remember how God took care of them in the ancient wilderness. These shelters help to remember and honor God's presence.

A temporary tent or shelter also reminds a Jewish mindset of temporary tabernacles built to house the presence of God. Peter wants to set up 3 shelters so Moses, Elijah, and Jesus can be honored. Why then is Peter considered parenthetically as brainless and obtuse? What exactly is the problem with Peter's construction proposal? Why does God cut short Peter's well-intentioned plan?

Peter is putting Jesus on the same level as Moses and Elijah. Like comparing a McDonald's filet of fish with a Ruth's Chris filet mignon, it's incomparable. God doesn't want multiple booths set up. Jesus is not equal to Moses and Elijah. Jesus is greater. There is no comparison. God is comparing Jesus to, well... uh, God. To the average Christian today, this seems like a no brainer. To first century Jewish folks like Peter, this is a revolutionary thought. Moses and Elijah sit atop the pinnacle of Jewish religious traditions for years. Moses and Elijah are it. There are none greater. Peter believes he is elevating Jesus up to the platforms of Moses and Elijah, and that being a good thing.

God breaks through Peter's good intentions and shows what is best. The words ascribed to God are interesting. He is pleased with His Son. Like a Jewish rabbi, God employs a teaching technique called remez. Remez takes a small piece of scripture to point to a greater whole. This rabbinical teaching technique doesn't work so well these days, but it was very effective with ancient Jewish people who had a command of Old Testament scripture. A few lines would enable a quick recall of a greater, complete passage of Bible text.

When God says, "This is my Son," this triggers Jewish people to think of Psalm 2, a prophetic verse concerning the Messiah. When God says, "...whom I have chosen," that references Isaiah 42 and another detailed prophecy concerning the Messiah. When God declares, "...listen to Him," ancient Jewish minds recall Deuteronomy 18:15. This is a key scripture pointing to the Messiah to be "like" Moses. God wants Peter and us to know that Jesus IS the Messiah. Jesus is it. Jesus is the fulfillment of Old Testament hopes. Jesus is to the brim with nothing lacking. He IS greater than Moses or Elijah combined, and therefore multiple booths just aren't an option.

I've set up multiple booths; have you? I don't mean to, but there they are. I want Jesus as Lord, but worries and checkbook often reflect differently. I have a well-built booth for my money and stuff. If time spent is any indication, then my career has a booth, my baseball card collecting has a booth, even my yard has a booth. Jesus does have a booth, but too often His is one among many.

According to what God said, there should be no comparison or competition with Jesus. How many booths do you have? Some will tell you multiple booths are just fine because Jesus is really only one of many ways to God. Jesus, some will claim, is certainly not God, but you might be. Go ahead and set up a special booth for yourself. Some believe they are Lord. Jesus said He was. What do you believe? Your answer will determine if "Christian" means Jesus follower or if "Christian" reflects a shallow self-help program and multiple booths. What do you believe about Jesus? Your view of God's Son will affect your worldview. Your worldview will determine how many booths or tents you set up in your backyard.

The Bible says Jesus is above all, through all, in all, and He holds everything together. (Colossians 1:15-17) Do you believe? A few years back, Louie Giglio was speaking at a major church conference when a science geek accosted him afterwards. The obvious chemistry major told Giglio he had to know about the glory of Laminin. Did Giglio know about Laminin? No. The excited laboratory buff proceeded to go off about Laminin. "Laminin holds everything together. It's the protein molecules in our bodies. They take one cell and attach to others. It's awesome, dude!" Giglio stood speechless and thankful he had finished high school biology. To help move this Laminin freak along, Giglio agreed to Google Laminin and check it out for himself. A guilt-driven Internet search later uncovered an amazing, Biblical truth attached to Laminin. The molecular structure of this protein is graphically displayed in the shape of the cross. Literally, Giglio began to believe, Jesus DOES hold all things together. He is incomparable. He is a one booth only kind of God.

Here's one last symbol or imagery from the transfiguration to consider. A cloud enveloped the mountain and shut down the prayer meeting. For

Jewish people, a cloud would have been reminiscent of God's Shekinah glory. God led His wilderness-dwelling people with a cloud of His glory during daylight hours. A cloud represented the presence of God. Sometimes that cloud or presence was so thick, people couldn't see their own toes.

Peter, James, and John are on a mountain with Jesus, Moses, and Elijah. A cloud engulfs them, and they are in the presence of God the Father. There's a sense within this dramatic scene that God is teaching: live in My presence and listen to My Son.

It's what Jesus's followers and authentic Christians do. They live in God's presence and listen to the Son. Living in the presence of God must go far beyond a few songs on Sunday morning. Living in His presence stretches to our family dinner times, our parenting, our jobs, our marriage, and to our money management. Living in the presence of God tempers you and directs you. His presence affects you, changes you, and transforms you. It transfigures you.

Living in the presence of God will impact the way you buy a car or house. Under your own convictions, you may not care what something costs because you've decided you deserve it. In the presence of God, you ask Him what you should or should not buy in light of others who have much less. Living in the presence of God changes our perspective on life. Real life. Your view of sex will change. The presence of God doesn't allow sex to be viewed as flippant, casual, or inconsequential. The presence of God demands sex be treated as an incredible gift designed for God's idea of marriage between a husband and wife. Anything short of this, and you're flying below the clouds of His presence. His presence brings life and blessings; the lack affords ruin and destruction.

People who live in the presence of God have a changed perspective because there's been a transformation. A transfiguration is not too strong a word for someone like Peter, James, John, you, and me who keep our heads in the cloud. Our thinking changes. Perspective and viewpoints change. Biblical and Godly worldviews begin to shape those who erect one booth and live in the presence of God.

Being transfigured in a disfigured world means perspectives are transformed. When perspectives are changed, living is also. Sex becomes a precious gift again. Life itself is honored and treasured. Scriptural morality is willingly lived out. Absolute truth begins to expose morality-lacking tolerance as the chaos it is. Os Guiness wrote, "People with a purely secular view of life have too much to live with, and too little to live for. Everything is permitted and nothing is important."[1] A transfigured Christian has reclaimed what's important.

For one final push, let's pull all the imagery of the transfiguration together into one concluding thought. Test and see if this equation can make sense in your life: After we commit (8 days), we get a glimpse of God (Mountain) and His fulfillment (Moses and Elijah) of being redeemed (Exodus) by only Jesus (3 shelters/tents). Consequently we should continue to live in God's presence and listen (cloud). THIS is how the transfiguration becomes meaningful for our marriages, families, finances, depression, addictions, dreams, churches, and service to a hurting world. Try the equation again. When you commit beyond the label of "Christian," God will reveal how you are fully equipped (to the brim) because of Jesus saving and living fully within you. Live all the areas of your life in God's presence, and listen to the active, guiding voice of Jesus. This powerful imagery changed Peter, James, and John. It can still affect change in us today. Your personal transfiguration will also transform power back into what it means to be a genuine Christian.

Chapter End Notes

1. Os Guinness, <u>The American Hour,</u> (New York, NY; Macmillan 1993) pg. 414.

Chapter Twelve

Fence Building

Strategy #12: Don't drive forward in reverse.

Luke 9:39-50

"The next day, when they came down from the mountain, a large crowd met him. A man in the crowd called out, "Teacher, I beg you to look at my son, for he is my only child. A spirit seizes him and he suddenly screams; it throws him into convulsions so that he foams at the mouth. It scarcely ever leaves him and is destroying him. I begged your disciples to drive it out, but they could not." "O unbelieving and perverse generation," Jesus replied, "how long shall I stay with you and put up with you? Bring your son here." Even while the boy was coming, the demon threw him to the ground in a convulsion. But Jesus rebuked the evil spirit, healed the boy and gave him back to his father. And they were all amazed at the greatness of God. While everyone was marveling at all that Jesus did, he said to his disciples, "Listen carefully to what I am about to tell you: The Son of Man is going to be betrayed into the hands of men." But they did not understand what this meant. It was hidden from them, so that they did not grasp it, and they were afraid to ask him about it. An argument started among the disciples as to which of them would be the greatest. Jesus, knowing their thoughts, took a little child and had him stand beside him. Then he said to them, "Whoever welcomes this little child in my

name welcomes me; and whoever welcomes me welcomes the one who sent me. For he who is least among you all—he is the greatest." "Master," said John, "we saw a man driving out demons in your name and we tried to stop him, because he is not one of us." "Do not stop him," Jesus said, "for whoever is not against you is for you."

Years ago I was a youth pastor. I wasn't a great one. Graciously, people somehow let me continue on this track for several years and learn. Teenagers always, always, always asked the burning question, "How far can I go?" If you're wondering if the underlying inquiry was about sex, you would be absolutely right. That was exactly what they were referring to. THAT was literally the burning question. Back seat, hormonal, animalistic, teenage, pre-marital sex could have and maybe should have been the topic of every Sunday night youth group. They wanted to know graphic details. Church kids wanted clearly defined boundaries concerning handholding, kissing, petting, necking and any new ING-ing that might pop up (I pity the fool youth pastors these days dealing with sexting!).

Truth be told, what raging teenage Christians were asking was this: How far can we go without falling off the edge of our faith? It was and remains the wrong question. Shouldn't there have been a push from the opposite direction to suggest how close to Jesus they could actually move? As a struggling youth pastor, I tried to put into place guidelines and safety nets --- fencing if you will --- to keep kids from falling off the edge. I pushed back on the teens' desire to stick their necks out in seeing how far down they would fall. With my push back, I would receive an expected shrug from their know-it-all shoulders and hear, "That's such a church answer." (sigh) Did I mention I wasn't a very good youth pastor? (more sigh)

Ancient rabbis did something similar to my teenage strategies. They would say, "We should build a fence around the Ten Commandments and Torah." The idea was to build a fence around God's Word and commands (no cheating, no lying, no adultery), so that there were stop-gaps before you fell off the edge of faith. Fencing in Torah kept people from falling out of relationship with God. The fence defined boundaries before they were crashed through by sin. Jesus built a fence around Torah too.

Jesus articulated how Jewish folks clearly understood and memorized Old Testament laws concerning things like murder and divorce. Those laws were part of Torah (Genesis, Exodus, Leviticus, Numbers, & Deuteronomy). Jesus would talk to hardcore Jewish believers and say, "You have heard that it was said long ago," as He launched into ideas about Torah commands. Then Jesus would begin to build His fence.

When Jesus referred to murder, Jesus pointed to hate being the same as murder. (Matthew 5:21-22) That was fence building. Before you fall off the edge of faith and physically kill someone, build a fence around your heart. Tinges of anger and hatred signal the need to begin building a safety wall of a white picket fence. Getting angry and calling someone a fool is fence building if you let it proactively signal a looming cliff.

Jesus did what ancient rabbis did a lot. Before people fell off the edge, they put up loving, pastoral fences. Jesus built a fence around marriage and commands concerning adultery. With an authority rarely found in first century rabbis, Jesus taught how looking and lusting was no different than a torrid, adulterous one-night stand. Can you see the fence Jesus firmly put in place to prevent folks from falling off the marriage ledge? Today, that fence is so consistently compromised, our kids are developing a sad, new normal.

Like a savvy rabbi, we are given an opportunity to build fence around the text of Luke 9. Our efforts will enable Christians to stop defaming the name of "Christian" and help keep Jesus's Church in progressive forward motion. For many, an effective church sounds like an oxymoron. There is a way for Christians to do church, and there is most definitely a way not to. So many have seen the way not to, and have left with little regard of returning. A little fence building might be necessary to turn things around.

Jesus very clearly articulates He wants to build His Church. (Matthew 16:18) Not my church. Not your church. Jesus is the head; we're the body. It's Jesus's Church. It's His bride. He wants to build the Church of Jesus Christ. That's a very good thing to remember as Dr. Luke moves us from a mountaintop event to a hard valley.

Finishing off a mountainous experience, Jesus and His friends venture back into real life with the less than spectacular hurting crowds. A father and his demon-possessed boy, prone to violent convulsions, beg for Rabbi Yeshua's help. Apparently some of Jesus's disciples had previously tried to cast the demon out, but got nothing. Desperation pushed the father and son to look for glimmers of hope, but any such chance would only be extinguished by another excruciating round of defeat. Failure from Jesus's followers did not help. A tired father is beginning to believe his young son's life might better be served if it could be cut short of more pain. With such a defeatist thought, he begins to doubt his very role of father. He's tried, but grief has left a trampled path of questions void of answers.

The disciples of Rabbi Jesus and those listening from the peripherals receive a pointed rebuke. Jesus makes a verbal note of an "unbelieving and perverse generation." Doesn't that sound a bit cranky? It seems the Son of God is getting weary of teaching, performing miracles, and people still not getting it. You sense a bit of a high and mighty attitude from Jesus. He's allowed; after all, He is high and mighty. Nonetheless, Jesus springs into action and heals the demonized boy. The Bible says He gave the son back to his father. Soak on that for a moment. Pause. Take an Old Testament "selah" moment. Jesus gives the son back, and people are amazed at God.

There is a way to do church that will prompt God to hand things back to us. The glory, aliveness, influence, and life of His Church can all be handed back to us. When God hands back His Church into our care, He also hands back our marriages, families, finances, and healing. We will be amazed.

Another Bible writer, Mark, expounds the same story of this demon-possessed child found in Mark chapter nine. Mark gives a few more details to consider. There are church people arguing in this version of the story. Most Christians are painfully aware of church people who argue. When church people argue, lost people lose. People who need healing lose when supposedly healed church folks begin to argue.

At the center of most church world arguments is the monster of "me." Let's just call it the way most non-believers see it: Me Church. John Hamby says, "People are strange. They like the front of the bus, the back of the church, and the center of attention."[1] Our human default is always on "me."

A huddle of religious leaders clashing with Jesus's followers proves Hamby's point to be a timeless one. The verbal fighting is symptomatic of the "me" monster rearing its selfish head. Churchy people fighting is never good and always selfish. Perhaps a fence is needed.

Jesus flashes divine authority when He zeroes in on the disciples and declares they are unbelieving. Some Bible translations use the word faithless. This is strong language aimed at believers --- believers who are unbelieving. These nine followers Jesus preaches at weren't included in a previous, miraculous, mountaintop experience. (Matthew 17:1) These nine stayed behind in the valley, and now Jesus deems their faith to be gone. Had they become too self-absorbed in their thinking and circumstances?

It's possible to focus so much on my valley that my faith disappears. It's also possible to do ministry and church my way so God is excluded. You and I can be so centered on "me" that our faith and God goes flying out the door. It's tough for faith to still be faith when our focus is selfish. Usually when we hole up in a self-centered cave, our faith becomes extremely inactive. Our faith and belief system can be shut down by the "me" monster. We can so easily become no good for no one when we fixate on number one. When this happens, faith isn't faith anymore. Faith without action towards God and others has completely flatlined. It's dead. (James 2:20)

When our church in Atlanta decides to go outside our walls on Sunday mornings, we chase away the "me" monster. We call these Sundays "FIA Sundays" (Faith In Action). Serving side-by-side beyond our normal Sunday morning confines makes life and church no longer about what I need, want, or get. We give these special Sundays over to poor, title one schools for supernatural makeovers. Our army of Jesus followers are able to restore brokenness as a visible act of the Gospel. Four to five times a year we intentionally shut down our church building so people are afforded an incredible opportunity to be the Church and serve. On these Sundays, we do church right. Some initially argued how church is not really church unless we're meeting in our building on a Sunday morning. I still remember the e-mail I received from a local pastor who found out what we were doing. Through a cowardly e-mail, he preached at me to repent. This kind of Sunday morning shenanigans was just wrong. It wasn't, in his thinking, church. I agreed. It was better. It was being the church. It put meaning behind our sign that said Cumberland COMMUNITY Church.

I believe our faith is not really faith unless there is some kind of action attached. Sitting, taking, and being fed in a climate-controlled environment doesn't take a whole lot of faith. On most Sunday mornings faith is not necessarily exercised. Closing down shop on Sunday mornings so the body can serve our community feels more like church than when we do church. On our FIA Sundays we experience worship, evangelism, prayer, community, service, teaching, and God. Everything we hope to happen within a long string of Sunday mornings happens deliberately and deeply on one FIA Sunday. It's doing church in a way that creates and builds Biblical faith.

Dr. Luke points to Jesus not only calling His friends faithless but also perverse. There's a nice little word you don't hear around the dinner table much. The idea of perverse tends to point towards sexual deviancy. I conjure up strange mental images of old, wild-haired men wearing random raincoats on a sunny, hot day. That's not what Jesus is saying. The word "perverse" in the Greek actually means "backwards." Jesus's disciples and a crowd of stuffy religious folks have turned the idea of Church completely backwards. When church becomes about us, it's backwards. When it's not about God and lost people, leadership is operating in reverse and the Kingdom moves backwards. How on earth can this kind of thing happen in a church?

When the goal of church shifts to what I can get out of it, church is moving backwards. Many corporate worship gatherings have morphed into hyper-active competitions of creating places where people are trained to receive. As Christians walk into a receiving sanctuary, an unspoken mantra proclaims, "Bless me, feed me, make me worship." We want our marriages fixed, our kids raised, and our offerings (tips might be a better word) used for what we think is best. Churches relentlessly meeting the needs of consumers have grown to monstrous and selfish proportions. When was the last time you and I walked into church looking for opportunities to give? How can we give ourselves in worship? How can we give ourselves to the kids' ministry? How can we give our money with no strings attached? How can we contribute to the teaching by giving alert, affirming head nods, and maybe even an occasional glimmer of participation with a spontaneous … uh, "Amen?" What is the focus of church for you? You can answer that question by listening to your own words immediately after the church service in the car ride home. Saying things like, "I really liked the music," or "I didn't get much out of the message," may indicate you have things backwards. But if you say, "I stood in the presence of God, and man… He was glorified today," you're moving away from being that perverted church guy in a trench coat. By the way, don't forget who is riding in the back seat listening to your enlightening conversations about church. It's the next generation who seem to be getting very tired of church. I wonder where that poor attitude is coming from?

Conversations after church, which point less to you and more to God, mean you're starting to get it. You're turning the corner. You're starting to turn the corner on Jesus's way of doing His Church. If a visitor taking your seat bugs you, a screaming baby makes you squirm, the offering causes a sigh, and you're not being served short of an oil change and gas money for the ride home --- you might just be driving in reverse.

Perhaps this "me" church rant sounds a bit ridiculous, and you feel the backwards label belongs to some other dying church down the road. Take another look. Consider how quick you and I can be offended in church world. For an entity founded on grace and unconditional love, I never cease to be amazed at how good we Christians are at holding grudges towards those in the same pew. We can quickly go down angry roads and begin processing how we'll quit our giving, quit our serving, or just plain quit. The quickness to quit or throw a religious tantrum is stunning. Most of the time, such junky church thinking is about me, me, and only me. Is this hitting too close to home? It is for me. What if, God forbid, a called leader believes and leads a campaign for change in your plateaued or dying church? Instead of trying to do the same, old, ineffective things better, this elected visionary might lean towards change and making things wonderfully uncomfortable. How would you deal with this? Backwards church people would rather fight than switch, and most often do.

There was an old cigarette commercial that had a rough cowboy sporting a black eye, and he would say, "I'd rather fight than switch." The marketing suggested people would rather take a punch to the face than change their beloved brand of cigarettes. Some would rather their church stay exactly the way it is because it's the way THEY like it. People would rather fight than switch the music. Many Christians would rather fight than switch programming, buildings, or even the place of the offering within the sacred order of worship. Are you able to determine how much of church is about you, and how much is about God? When did the goal of maintaining something I like override the effectiveness of the gospel and unleashing the bride of Christ? What do you demand for yourself, and what do lost people need that will require dying to those same demands?

It's somewhat ironic how assurance in Christ can give us self worth, but yet our caution is to not focus on self. Our identity and self-worth found in Jesus can free us to forget about our needs so we can love others God places around us. That's so much easier for me to write than live. There are many potential selfish pitfalls trying to be a Christian in church world. It's almost as if our Sunday default is backwards. What did Jesus do with His backwards followers?

Jesus had commissioned His committed friends to work with great power and authority. (Matthew 28:18) Twisted backwards, however, the disciples were dis-abled to heal a demon-possessed boy. Hmm... they were supposed to be able to do this.

What was going on? Jesus's followers had been given tremendous potential, and yet nothing happened with this enslaved little boy. Why couldn't they heal this boy since Jesus had given them supernatural clout to do so? Backwards selfish thinking handcuffed Jesus's followers into believing they could handle it all on their own. It was the problem of more "me."

Ancient Jewish people thought they could exorcise demons without God's help. With a few wild dandelion roots stuck up people's nostrils, perverse religious folks believed they could take on Satan's demons. It didn't work.

An out of balance perspective on self inflates our sense of personal empowerment. A false sense of competency, nevertheless, enables us to work and move like things can be handled all on our own. Are we able to do church all on our own? Are we THAT good? Can selfish people grow a successful church without God's help? Is it possible to fill up a church building without God? If we can, then we are prayerless. If we are prayerless, we are powerless. It's such a wild dichotomy to understand how good we've become at filling up our church buildings on Sunday mornings and yet remain prayerless and powerless. On our own, we will be powerless to heal, powerless to change, powerless to receive back from God, and powerless to fight the fiery demons of hell dogging you and me.

Jesus explains how demons could only come out with prayer and fasting. (Mark 9:29) Jesus is showing His narcissistic friends how they are blindly operating under their own ego-boosting cognizance. Their selfish focus is robbing them of power. They didn't pray. They didn't fast. They had no power.

When we are full of ourselves, we're usually empty of prayer and power. Prayer takes us several steps beyond ourselves, but fasting elevates our circumstances to a whole new level of unselfish behavior. Fasting shows God our intensity to go beyond ourselves. Someone once said, "Prayer attaches you to heaven. Fasting detaches you from the world and yourself." The fast track for backwards churches to get back on track is prayer and fasting. The monster of "me" cannot co-exist in a body that has prayer and fasting in its DNA. You want to do church right? Cancel the church conference registration. Instead, begin walking the seats on Sunday mornings and crying out for Jesus to build His Church His way. Start praying and fasting, and asking a few others to join you. You'll be amazed.

Jesus heals the demon-possessed boy, and curious gawkers are amazed at God. While folks are caught with their mouths dropped, Jesus wants to say something very important to His friends. If Jesus says, "Listen carefully to what I am about to tell you," you should probably get out of the La-Z-Boy and pay close attention. Jesus whispers to His friends that He will be betrayed into rebellious hands.

The disciples don't get it. They are clueless about any type of betrayal. Jesus is referring to suffering, sacrifice, and a cross looming in the near future. Close friends don't understand Jesus's words. Meaning is hidden, and embarrassment keeps them from asking for clarity. An inward concentration blocks their understanding. The disciples are engrossed with power, position, influence, greatness, and receiving. They are focused on a coming political kingdom to satisfy their "me" factor. Their backwards drive for what they want blinds them to surrounding needs requiring sacrifice and an eventual rugged cross.

This selfish thinking forces Jesus into building some fence. He needs to teach and help His disciples be proactive in doing and being the Church. It is no time too soon either. The self-centered disciples begin arguing about why Peter got front row tickets to the transfiguration. Who picked James and John to go? Those two brothers are nothing but power and control freaks, and you should see their mother! Have you seen their mom? Please. She should have her own reality TV show --- "Real Housewives of Israel."

Do you see what's happening here? If you look closely, you might think you're looking into a ding-dang mirror. Have you found yourself in similar churchy arguments about who's right, what's right, and your right to be right? That way of doing church quickly degenerates into selfish and crazy behavior.

My wife has a laundry list of church weirdness and selfish behavior. Over the years, people feeling the power of self have confronted Sherry with sheer stupidity exactly because she is the pastor's wife. One woman felt the need to tell my wife she was a little too skinny and wondered if she was struggling from anorexia. Oh man, I can still remember Sherry's nostrils flaring as she wanted to fire back, "And aren't you a little too FAT?" Wow. She didn't, and I kept my job. When the "me" monster shows up, things get ugly. I love what Jesus does with all of this. He grabs a child for an object lesson. Is it the same child who was previously convulsing from demon possession? A calm, angelic, haloed child stands beside Jesus and becomes a living illustration for how His church should really function.

In the first century, a child had no power or authority. They had no semblance of influence. Parents could not be sued. Stoning outside city gates proved to be extremely preventative. Kids were completely helpless during Jesus's day. Jesus explains how kids are a great reminder of the way we are to do church. The Bible writer, Matthew, writes how Jesus urges believers to actually become more like little kids, because kids represent the greatest among us.

When a child becomes the standard for greatness, doesn't that put everyone in the same class? If a little knee nipper is great, the search for greatness among mature folks becomes unnecessary. If kids are the measure of greatness, adults probably shouldn't concern themselves with position, power, and influence any longer. If kids are great, then so are widows, orphans, poor people, sick and helpless people. This kind of thinking would revolutionize the way we do and the way we ARE the Church.

Growing up, my most awesome youth minister was Bob Smith. Bob was the coolest youth minister ever. He sported lamb chop sideburns. He drove a black GTO with a color organ built into his dashboard. When his solid state FM radio was blaring, the lights would flash and dance. Bob used to drive really fast in his gas guzzling GTO; in 1968 it didn't matter because petrol was a magnificent 25 cents per gallon. Over the years, Bob made numerous trips hauling me back and forth to a church camp some two hours away. Bob also drove a black, Honda motorcycle. This very hip, cool youth minister would come over to my house when I was eight years old. He would hang out with me. He coached my little league team. Some forty years later I wonder why Bob did those things. Maybe he needed to. Did Bob need a reminder that Church was not about him? Was a wide-eyed, eight-year-old fan all he needed to remember his calling and church was not about position, power, or influence?

Between 2005 and 2007, the incredible state of Colorado afforded me a much too brief time of ministry. While teaching in a place called Highlands Ranch, I literally ran into a young man in his mid-to-late 20's almost every Sunday morning. We'll call him "David" to grant a bit of protection. David had some social and mental capabilities comparable to a young child.

Before weekend services, David would blindside me with bear hugs and love bumps while I tried to converse with other church goers. Sometimes David would bump me across the room and out of breath. I'm pretty sure it was his awkward way of expressing love and appreciation. He viewed me as his friend. One day I took David to lunch; I bought him whatever he was hungry for, and I worked at keeping awkward conversation alive. I think David enjoyed the time, but it was especially good for my soul.

The very next day, another pastor inquired who I had taken to lunch the day before. I gladly dropped

David's name. "Why did you take HIM to lunch?" replied my cynical coworker. Admittedly, I was a bit befuddled by his harsh remarks. My fellow pastor went on to say, "You can't hang out with people like that. You are a leader, and you have to focus on other leader-type people." I was speechless as he continued to hammer home his point. "I learned long ago that I cannot afford to spend time with such people. There are people of influence, there are people of wealth, and there are people of leadership who I must focus on." These words still reverberate within me years later. I want to live and do church the exact opposite way of my backwards friend.

When I'm focused only on the leaders, the wealthy, and the influential, I've usually got an eye out for what I can receive. These slanted conversations are most often about MY agenda or MY church. The darkness in my selfish heart never ceases to amaze me. Jesus, on the other hand, prompts me to hang with people who are okay attributing greatness to little kids.

Our Children's Pastor, Jen, believes everyone should serve in the kids' ministry area. Jen wants passionate adults who love kids to serve with her, but she thinks everyone should fit this criterion because kids are great.

Maybe Jen's idea is a good one; maybe we should mandate everyone to serve in the nursery, kids, or teen ministries. Would such initiative build a fence around our churches and hearts? Would this remind us that church isn't about me? Before we're pushed off the edge by the "me" monster, wouldn't serving little kids be good for our hearts and humility? Changing a diaper or two could humbly remind us of Jesus's definition of greatness.

Our story from Luke nine finishes with Jesus's close, egocentric disciples complaining. They're not liking someone else doing ministry who isn't attached to their elite group. Good thing we don't have to deal with such religious competiveness in our day. How silly. Just because Jesus's friends can't cast out a demon or two, they're upset with someone who can. Ridiculous ancient history, right?

Jewish people in the first century were really good at dividing. They were known to be very sectarian. Followers would huddle around a rabbi and what the rabbi believed. They would huddle around theologies. Whatever certain rabbis believed about divorce, so would a tightly knit group of disciples. Groups would be shaped by opinions concerning when a Passover meal should be served. There were huddling, dividing, and religious walls formed by driving desires to be right while proving others horribly wrong. Jesus's friends were no different. They were the ones hand-picked by the Messiah. The Apostles were the elite huddle group who traveled and lived with Rabbi Jesus. They were officially commissioned to do ministry in His name. Who was this other guy trying to cast out a demon in Jesus's name? He wasn't a part of their holy huddle! He wasn't a part of their church.

There's very little application for us, right? We're not wall builders. We don't divide. For us, "sectarian" is a past, dusty, irrelevant word. We've moved beyond the poor attitudes of Jesus's disciples.

We're an advanced species of modern day church folk aficionados. We know better than those silly siloed disciples.. Let's list the names of a few churches. I'd bet the ranch you and I aren't affiliated with every one of these: Baptist. Methodist. Presbyterian. Saddleback. Willow Creek. Northpoint. How can all those other churches say they're doing things in Jesus's name when they're not my church? They're not a part of my denomination. How can Jesus empower them and me at the same time? My methodology and my theology is different than theirs. All of this just doesn't make good church sense to me. Did you happen to count the overt usage of "me" and "my" in those last few lines? If so, you see the problem.

The application to our current church world is, perhaps, somewhat understated. It's dreadfully ironic that we serve one Lord, but fight each other. In one church or in one city, we still fight each other. How can we build some fence? What can we do to keep Jesus's church from becoming mine? How can we do church so Jesus will give back influence, glory, life, and the faded name of "Christian" to faithful church goers?

Community groups might be a good place to start. Small groups, not holy huddles, can begin to build some fence around Jesus's Church. What's the difference between a small group and a holy huddle? Holy huddles work on remaining sectarian, rigid, and right. Small groups welcome diversity… even kids. In a good small group, you will face decisions to accept people who aren't like you. A beer in someone's hand will challenge you with the one purposely not in yours. A couple's parenting style will contradict yours. Your comfort zones will be all funked up by a good community group. Here's the way it will unfold for you.

For a couple of months, your new small group will go fairly well. Relationships will begin and remain somewhat on a safe surface. At some sudden point, there will be a sonic soul boom. That will be the sound of real life unfolding. It might be a marriage crisis, a huge career decision, a gut-wrenching miscarriage, an unrelenting sin, or maybe even a relational problem within group dynamics. Somebody at some point will open up and share. They will demand more from your group than chips and dip. One person's conflict will risk vulnerability. Everyone else in the group will have to choose if they'll put naked toes in the waters of community or not. How do I know this? I'm not actually a prophet. I've simply experienced these kinds of defining moments time and time again. You might find yourself saying, "Holy cow! What the heck? I didn't bargain for this." The group you've signed up for is about to go through the tunnel of chaos. M. Scott Peck writes about this in his book, "The Road Less Traveled." Pseudo community and authentic community can be separated by the amount of difficulty endured or not. You can choose to leave, or you can choose to go through the tunnel. It's not an easy thing, and many Christians bent on selfish comfort choose not to. If you decide to go through the tunnel of chaos with budding friendships, you'll find a deeper sense of community, relationship, and acceptance on the other side. You will have learned how to deal with circumstances and personalities unlike your own, and THAT is exactly how you do Jesus's church.

A community group built on the designs of Jesus will teach you how greatness (like kids) is more about accepting than asserting. It's more about relinquishing power than gaining it. Greatness comes when people who aren't like you figure out how to do life with you --- and you with them. Small groups transform. Small groups change us from "me" to "we" to God. Community groups can be great fence building to keep the Church in Jesus's hands and out of ours.

Could your life or church use some spiritual fence building? The "me" monster wreaks church world havoc especially with those who desperately need to get in. There is a way to do church without falling off an evil, egotistical edge. There is a way to give and receive back vitality, life, glory, influence, effectiveness, and healing in our churches. Your prayers and fasting, perspective of greatness, and ability to embrace others become key components. Give it a shot. All the cool, real Jesus followers are doing it. They're also the ones reclaiming "Christian" with power to BE Jesus's Church. That's how do to church!

Chapter End Notes

1. Hamby, John, <u>Sermon: "Classic Problems That The Disciples Faced"</u>, (Vilonia, AK; First Baptist Church 2002).

Chapter Thirteen

Tiny Pretzels

Strategy #13: Remember, size DOES matter!

Luke 13:18-20
"Then Jesus asked, "What is the kingdom of God like? What shall I compare it to? It is like a mustard seed, which a man took and planted in his garden. It grew and became a tree, and the birds perched in its branches." Again he asked, "What shall I compare the kingdom of God to?"

I like tiny pretzels. You can buy a whole pound for less than a couple bucks. Give me a bag of tiny pretzels, and I'll quickly grab a squirt bottle of yellow mustard (or sometimes a tub of cream cheese if I'm feelin' crazy). Tiny pretzels and mustard will invariably beckon a host of angels singing the Hallelujah Chorus over my comfy couch outpost. Oh yeah.

Eating these miniature delights prompts me to hunger for an even bigger favorite: Mall pretzels. Those are the absolute best. I believe YOU know exactly what I'm talking about. Have you noticed how mall pretzels are marketed with such savvy methods? Bite-sized pretzel samples are given wonderfully free. The alluring smell of freshly baked pretzels sucks you into actually purchasing one. Oh man. I carry a frequent-buyer pretzel punch card because I'm so weak. If there's anything I like better than tiny pretzels, it's the giant mall pretzels smothered in plastic pouched mustard. Mall pretzels are better because they are bigger. Bigger is always better. You know this to be unquestionably true as well.

For 50 more cents, you can super-size your combo meal. "Would you like to super-size that?" is a no-brainer. A couple quarters more gets you twice the food and drink of other less intelligent consumers. Who wouldn't super size? Bigger is always better.

Just before my wife and I became health food freaks, we watched a film documentary called *Super Size Me*. If you like golden arches, you shouldn't watch this movie. The movie begins with the main character, Morgan Spurlock, getting a clean bill of health from a credible doctor. The movie unfolds documenting the next 30 days of this very healthy, 32-year-old man eating only at McDonalds. Breakfast, lunch, and supper were all served by a red-haired clown asking the question, "Would you like to super-size that?" Every time a cashier asked this question, the answer was yes. He said, "Yes," every time because bigger is better. During the movie, Spurlock also limited his physical activity to less than 5,000 steps per day to mimic a sad, American lifestyle.

At the end of his deep-fried 30 days, Morgan was told he was dying. A greatly concerned physician insisted Spurlock stop his diet and begin an aggressive exercise program. After a month of super sizing, Spurlock's cholesterol was off the charts, his liver was shutting down, and depression was setting in. "Bigger is better" began sounding more like something the grim reaper would say as a dinner guest.

Is bigger always better?

Jesus dealt with religious folks who believed bigger is better. Pharisees, high priests, and other Jewish leaders leaned towards the large and powerful. This was exactly why they rejected Jesus as the Messiah. The Messiah had to be larger than life itself. Bigger. The Messiah had to come in power and with flash, and would kick some Roman butt. The promised One had to have military, political, economic, and social clout. Jesus didn't seem to fit the bio because He wasn't decidedly bigger. My superior attitude immediately writes these old religious dudes off as cheese bombs. They were idiots. How could they be so close and be so incredibly off the mark?

I do the same thing. Idiot. When a church is defined by it's massive buildings, culturally relevant architecture, spotlighted pastor, and a packed parking garage, I'm quick to declare God's mighty hand at work with such obvious evidence. Bigger programs, bigger ministries, bigger budgets, and bigger bands are always better, right? Isn't much of our thinking similar to the Jewish folks who turned their noses up at Jesus?

Jesus responds to all of this nonsense with a calm, "That's not how I roll." This isn't how His Kingdom works. What IS it like? It's like a mustard seed.

Jesus is so good at taking every day, common objects, and teaching the details of His Kingdom. He uses camels, gates, doors, money, and tiny, little mustard seeds. From 20 feet away, you cannot see the mustard seed I hold in my hands. That's part of the very large point.

If you plant a mustard seed, how would you do it? Even without much horticulture background, you and I would dig a small hole, place the seed gently into the ground, cover with rich top soil, and water. That's how you plant. But when Jesus talks about planting a mustard seed, He uses the Greek word "ballo" for "planted." Ballo means throw. In fact, "ballo" is actually throwing something off to the side without concern for where that something lands. Balloing is tossing something into obscure margins and confidently moving on.

Dr. Luke continuously points us to the word "seed" being synonymous with the Bible. We touched on this idea in chapter six as Jesus taught using dirt. If you throw out a little bit of Bible seed, something is going to happen. Take a small piece of God's Word and toss it in any direction. Something is going to happen. Place a tiny, almost unidentifiable seed of God's Word into unlikely hands, and you'll be amazed at the results. The Word is one in the same as Jesus. Jesus is the Word, and the Word is Jesus. (John 1:1) Jesus is seed, and He'll be living and active no matter where He's flung.

I know some will claim they've got nothing to offer the Kingdom. They've not been to Bible College. They don't have scripture memorized, and, perhaps, have a very green, new faith. Is there really anything significant such a person can do for God? Really? Remember, in the real Kingdom, bigger isn't always better.

Can you recite John 3:16 if a pastoral gun is put to your head? Even if recollection is attached to a macaroni plaque made in a third grade VBS class, do you remember these classic words? We've kept this incredible verse stored safely in our kids' ministry departments. We pat little heads and congratulate them for gaining a lifetime membership to the 3:16 Club. We should stop doing this. In fact, you should try saying them out loud right now. Come on, nobody's looking. Can you do it? "For God so loved the world that He gave his one and only Son, that whoever believes in Him shall not perish but have eternal life." It felt good, didn't it? And now you have no excuse, my friend. You are a Kingdom player with a mustard seed in your back pocket. You have a little seed in your hands. Throw it out there. Toss these words in any direction, and watch what God does. That's how the Kingdom rolls.   God has an uncanny way of taking the very small and building something large and lasting. That's how He wants to use you and me.

On a mundane Friday in 2005, Joel McDonald walked into my office. I was finishing up my sermon for the weekend, and was trying desperately to keep my office door closed for the duration. Regardless, Joel barged in. My sermon was of no concern to this curly-headed high school kid. His starting position on the local basketball team was. Joel was a senior point guard playing in the basketball crazed town of Washington, Indiana. In Washington, varsity basketball players were treated as local gods --- especially if they were winning.

With a home game unfolding that night, a red-faced Joel explained, "*I quit! I'm tired of Coach Omer. I can't take it. He yells at me all the time. I can't play for the man. I quit.*" As important as my sermon was, losing our starting point guard and the night's home game seemed to trump anything I was doing. I sprung into pastoral counseling mode and suggested Joel and I go play some tennis. Weird, I know --- but I was operating on the fly. We had a tennis court mapped out in the gym/auditorium of our church. I grabbed a few balls, a couple rackets, and headed to the auditorium. Truth be known, I was making all of this up as I went. I needed Joel out of my office and back on the basketball court as soon as possible. A stress-relieving game of tennis might be the trick I needed.

I threw Joel a couple tennis balls and said, "Joel, picture the face of Coach Omer on the tennis ball. Now hit it like you really want to hit it!" I realize now this wasn't the most loving, pastoral advice I could give, but I DID have a sermon to get back to. Joel smacked the ball so hard it hit the back wall and ricocheted towards my head. I simply wanted to clear Joel's head of his immediate frustrations.

A few whacks later, Joel seemed to be settling down. I wasn't sure what my next brilliant idea would look like, and so I prayed, "Lord, give me something for this kid." I grabbed another bright, fluorescent tennis ball and told Joel the plan. "Joel," I said, "I'm going to be at the game tonight. Don't quit. When I see Coach Omer riding you, I want you to look up into the stands. I'm going to be standing up holding this bright, green tennis ball. When you see me standing like a dork with a tennis ball, you'll know I'm praying for you. Don't quit!"

That night, the first half of basketball was awful. Joel was playing like he had hurt himself playing tennis earlier (yikes!). He was not having a good game. When our team came out of the locker room to warm up for the second half, the entire team was hanging their heads in presumed defeat. Coach Omer had obviously lit the team up. I stood in the stands with my tennis ball. Joel looked up into the stands of the 5,000-seat Hatchet House and found me. He gave me a slight, jock nod of recognition. Joel went on to have his best half of basketball the town had seen. Our team won, and Joel was named player of the game.

Before the next game, Joel opened his gym locker, and hundreds of tennis balls spilled out. Somehow our little deal had leaked to the cheerleader press. Word began to leak out at our church, and in the small town of 12,000. All kinds of people were showing up at basketball games with tennis balls. It was very strange. This went on until some supposed unsaved person threw one of the tennis balls onto the court during a game. At this point, the announcer man stopped play and told everyone to stop bringing tennis balls to the basketball games. It was an embarrassing moment for me, to say the least. This unfortunate incident, however, didn't stop the ground swell of fans who wanted to keep our team motivated. T-shirts with bright green tennis balls starting flying off local silk-screen printers. The backs of these tennis ball t-shirts sported Philippians 4:13: "I can do all things through Christ who strengthens me."

Unbelievably, our local basketball team won their league. They won sectionals, and conquered regionals. The Washington Hatchets grabbed the semi-state title, and headed for the state championship in Indianapolis. We won all the high school basketball marbles with a last-second, half-court shot from 7-footer, Luke Zeller. It was our real-life movie version of Hoosiers.

Am I saying I accomplished all of this with a little tennis ball? YES! No… not really, but you never know what God will do when you employ a little seed He's placed in your hands. It's how His Kingdom works. A mustard seed becomes a powerful symbol of inclusion for people like you and me who don't always feel very significant.

A tiny mustard seed has the ability to grow into a tree shooting up 10-12 feet high. In the Middle East, mustard trees become havens for birds and animals to find shade and rest. All from such tiny, miniscule seeds no bigger than the ink from this following period.

In the Middle East, however, people don't like mustard seed trees. They're nuisance plants. They're prickly scrub shrub. A mustard seed tree gets in the way and is deemed ugly by locals. This is exactly the kind of "foolish" stuff God chooses to propagate His Kingdom. Isn't this the same reason so many people got sucked into the phenomenon called American Idol?

When we watch *American Idol*, and some still do, we see little nobodies take the stage. There are 16-year-old unknowns who give it a shot. Twenty-somethings who have all but given up, muster one more dose of hope. I love those early rounds of whackos who really do think they can sing (it's the dark part of me)! Some Idol contestants are written off by bloggers as nuisances and creatively ugly. After weeks of survival, we watch young singers turn into stars. Lumps of coal squeezed into gems creating new music careers and entertainment for us. Carrie Underwood, Kelly Clarkson, Chris Daughtry, Jennifer Hudson, and Phillip Phillips are good examples. It's an incredible cultural phenomenon when you think about it.

God has a supernatural ability to make something significant from something insignificant in any culture. God can use YOU to be substantial rest and shade for hurting people. You have a little seed in your hand. You're a Kingdom recruit. That's the point of Jesus holding out a mustard seed. Are you feeling any better about your possibilities? Maybe you're a mustard seed. Maybe you're holding a small seed in your hand. Either way, you're a player.

Rabbi Jesus follows up His mustard seed object lesson with a second parable using yeast. Often times ancient rabbis would use two, back-to-back stories to make one very good point. Yeast becomes Jesus's next tool for teaching. Ancient Jewish rabbis would attach both positive and negative connotations to yeast. To make rising, leavened bread, ancient Jewish folks would take a small ball of bread dough and place it off to one side of the kitchen to leverage the leavening/yeast process. The tiny dough ball was considered contaminated as the yeast would grow. That small piece of dough would be placed into a new batch of dough made the next day to contaminate the entire new bowl of bread dough. The contaminated dough ball would cause new dough to rise. Making bread rise was a good thing. On the other side of the yeast coin, however, the symbol pointed to sin. That was a bad thing. Yeast, therefore, had good and bad implications.

Jesus says things like, "The yeast of the Pharisees can infiltrate your life." A first-century Jewish person would hear Rabbi Jesus say this and immediately wonder, "Is this good or bad?" Have you ever wanted Jesus to spell something out very clearly without you having to worry, doubt, question, or sometimes think? "Jesus, is yeast good or bad? Is a little, contaminated dough ball a good thing or not? Just tell me!"

Along with the yeast parable, Jesus's story tells about a woman who mixed a large amount of flour and dough. How much was she mixing? Approximately three seahs worth of flour were flying in her kitchen. One seah was about 50 pounds worth. That's a lot flour. That's ten bags of our grocery store standard.

The first century Jewish mind would have heard Jesus say "three seahs" and immediately think of an Old Testament passage. Because most Jewish people had the entire Old Testament memorized by age 13, certain connecting phrases would be triggers for their awesome Biblical literacy. Three seahs would flip mental, Jewish rolodexes to Genesis 18:6 and Abraham.

Abraham was visited by angels and wanted his wife, Sarah, to pull together three seahs of flour and make some bread. What do you order out when angels show up? Apparently a lot of bread. Abraham proved it was a very good thing to welcome and feed angels.

Jesus says His Kingdom resembles a little bit of yeast mixed into 150 pounds of flour. This, I think, is a positive comment concerning yeast. This is a good thing. A lot of flour can be influenced and positively contaminated by a little dough ball of yeast. Jesus is underlining His point: God produces significance from the insignificant. This is a very good thing. This is a great big thing.

Why does God operate like that? Why does He favor the small? Why on earth would heaven come down wrapped in an infant's blanket? Why didn't God wait for David to grow up before he undertook the manly challenge of killing Goliath? Why were thousands fed with a small boy's skimpy lunch? God has a long track record of choosing unlikely candidates to change His world. He picked a small handful of ragamuffin disciples to first lead His Church. Why on earth would a God in heaven decide to use someone like you and me?

Here's the short answer: Because it brings glory to God, and keeps Him on His rightful throne and off of our stolen ones. Often times the banner of Christian is linked to our own ideas of power, wealth, and an unhealthy grandiosity. *I am going to become a mighty oak tree for You, God!* Whether it's a church or an individual, I believe Jesus responds with, "But I need a mustard seed. I want to create scrub bushes for rest and shade. Those ugly nuisances bring Me glory, not agricultural accolades." That's the way His Kingdom works. God chooses the foolish things, the smaller things, and the insignificant things to convict and confound a bigger and better world. (I Corinthians 1:27)

Dallas Willard calls this a divine conspiracy.[1] It doesn't make a whole lot of sense to our over stimulated senses, but it does keep us from boasting, forgetting God, or trying to steal away His glory for our own. Jesus followers are OK being small. Many "Christians" pursue the absolute best and biggest they can be. Being individually significant, for many, is more appealing than watching a big God ultimately define what living large should really look like.

Let's name a few significant people. Bill Gates is a good starting point. Martha Stewart usually graces top ten lists of heavy hitters. Add Steven Spielberg, Simon Cowell, and Harry Potter author, J.K. Rowling. We could throw in a Bush and an Obama to balance things out. Oh… and let's name-drop Peyton Manning again because he formerly quarterbacked God's team. What if such names comprised your team roster and you were the project manager on NBC's new show, "The Christian Apprentice?" Donald Trump is about to assign your dream team a massive, Biblical undertaking.

This team of unbelievable, high capacity people possesses all the resources necessary to make things happen. This is a mover-shaker group of leaders. If the above folks are your team, there's no way you'll get fired. Well… unless Trump holds out his hand and asks you to make, "One of these." Upon leaning closer to the Donald, you see he's holding a tiny mustard seed. You immediately know you'll be fired on the spot. Your team is big. Your team is great, but they can't make a seed with the unlocked potential of becoming a 12-foot tree offering unconditional shade and rest. Your team is good, but not that good. They're not that big. I can see Peyton hanging his head in defeat as he shuffles out the boardroom. God is the opposing team and sits with a confident smile. Interestingly, He has characteristics reminiscent of George Burns and Morgan Freeman. Weird. A mere mustard seed is a piece of cake for this project manager. That's just the way His Kingdom works. He creates and uses small, tiny things packed with potential. AND, if you throw them out there, you won't believe what He'll do with them.

Do you know what a CFL is? Many green homes are using CFL's. Soon they'll be the new standard. Compact Fluorescent Lights use 75-80% less energy than traditional light bulbs. Although new CFL's cost more, if 110 million American households would use just one, we would create enough reserve energy to power a city of 1.5 million people. We would have enough power for the state of Delaware and Rhode Island combined. All of this with just one CFL per American home. One little light bulb.

Every American household using one CFL is the equivalent to taking 1.3 million polluting cars off the

roads. All we have to do is install one CFL light bulb.
Never underestimate the power of small.

A few summers back, our church put on a kid's
camp with a rock and roll theme. We invited
neighborhood, apartment complex, and latchkey kids
to come. At the end of our rockin' week, we gave
away two electric guitars. One was given to a girl, and
one to a boy. There was a particular boy who came
from a poor, single-parent home. He could only dream
of winning the guitar. His family lived well below the
governmental lines of poverty. He never had much,
and never expected to get much. He sure did want that
guitar though. Somehow (and I think I know how)
this kid won the blue, electric guitar. All our adult
volunteers were just as excited. They saw how cool
God was in providing a blue guitar for a hurting kid
through a random drawing from an old hat. The value
and love God poured into that kid through a guitar was
a sight to see. Where did the guitar come from? An
anonymous donor decided to make a small
contribution to our camp with the shiny, new
instruments. Who knows what God will do with one
kid's life because someone donated a guitar to give
away? Don't underestimate the power of small.

I like to ask new people coming into our church
what they like best. Is it the music? What about the
kids' and teen ministries? Is it…is it… my messages?
Not that I gain value, self-worth, or identity from such
a shallow thing as that. I hate that kind of pastor.
Sigh. So… is it my messages (I need to know!)?
Nope. Ouch. What people consistently comment on
is our food and coffee offered before our services. Are

you kidding me? A few people brew pots of coffee and bake some breakfast goodies. That's it? Can you believe this? I put in twenty-five plus hours each week on my sermons, and people like the java and monkey bread. Unbelievable. Here's what new people have told me: "When you're a new person coming into this place, it's a little intimidating. You don't know other people. When we went to the table with food and coffee, we started talking with people we never knew. We were grabbing coffee, and they were sharing the sugar and passing the banana nut bread. THAT was the best thing ever." Never underestimate the power of small.

God takes the insignificant and makes the significant. Christians who brag about Sunday attendances may not get this, but Jesus followers sure do. When I traveled to Kenya, I met Mama Milka. She is a mom of seven kids. Her youngest is six months old. Her oldest daughter is 23. Mama Milka's husband is AWOL supposedly looking for work. When he does stumble back home, Mama Milka usually becomes pregnant again. She lives in a 10x30 lean-to hut. To feed her family, she picks greens and kale in perilous fields filled with black mamba poisonous snakes. Her work begins in the early morning hours and lasts long into the day.

My wife and I decided to send monthly support to Mama Milka. You need to know the amount we sent per month was less than it takes to fill our van up with gas. When we sent Mama Milka an initial check of 6 months support, she immediately began praising God. She prayed for Sherry and me. She had been sick and didn't have enough money to see a doctor. The doctor she went to was not a lead physician of an outstanding HMO like we might demand. Mamma Milka saw a doctor we wouldn't take our sick cat to. However, she saw a doctor, and was able to buy the necessary medicine to get better and tend to her family once again.

But that wasn't all. Mama Milka explained she also was able to buy a big sack of rice and big sack of beans. She could now start selling the grains and begin her dream of owning a roadside business. She could get out of the dangerous kale fields. Mama Milka could stop relying on her five-year-old to take care of her six-month-old because Mama would be able to be home more. I am not a big, fat missions financier. Sherry and I gave pitifully small amounts to Mama Milka. It was embarrassingly small. However, like the potential locked in to a small seed, it's amazing what God can do when we make our resources available no matter what size. Don't underestimate the power of small. One child in Kenya can go to school an entire year for $150. That's less than some will spend on movies, eating out, or their cable bundle. Don't underestimate the power of small. What big story will you begin writing when you give your small contribution?

To make a living illustration of God's divine conspiracy of small, we gave out starter bags of Amish friendship bread one Sunday morning to all who gathered for church. From one starter bag, people were supposed to make three other starter bags to give away. They were also supposed to make two loaves of bread, giving one away and eating the other one. The stories we shared and the friends we made were so very cool. Who knew the power of this simple Amish experiment?

After the stories poured in, I played a game of "what if" with our church. "Let's just say," I explained, "that Jenn shared a loaf of bread with a lonely elderly woman." I asked my audience to help paint this scenario. What if… this woman was lonely because her husband had died and kids moved away. Often times our elderly don't lose faith, they just seldom get encouraged. What if… Jenn gave her loaf of bread to this older widow who minutes before was thinking, "I think I'd rather be dead and in heaven than alive and lonely." Just then the doorbell rang to signal Jenn, her smile, and a homemade loaf of bread. The bread and short visit reminded a lonely woman how God still loves her. The bread reminded her that Jesus is her bread of life. The apartment door closed and brought Jenn's visit to an end. But the woman got a phone call from her grandson who was struggling with his mom and dad's potential divorce. He wanted to leave home, but grandma's talk seemed to be just the soothing salve he needed to find a bit of peace in the storm. That grandson went to school the very next day and encountered one of his young biology teachers struggling to keep his head above water as a first year high school teacher. This new teacher had his written resignation in his briefcase, but a resolved grandson was able to encourage his teacher to stick it out the rest of the year. And on and on and on we go.

Could this really happen from a loaf of Amish friendship bread? Yes, and it did.

I challenge people to look for Zacchaeus coming into our church. Such people seem to be pouring in these days. These are people a little short on self-esteem, hated by some, seldom called by their real name, and willing to climb a tree for a little hope. You can spot a Zacchaeus ten pews away by their empty eyes. They've strolled into church because they don't know where else to turn. Life is hard. Maybe church will offer some hope and help. They've heard this can still happen on a Sunday morning. Driving down I-75 and into our parking lot, Zacchaeus people have a common, purposeless stare found all over Atlanta. Have you driven in rush hour traffic and notice similar gazes? They're ready to give in and give up. Their marriage has sunk. Perhaps bad financial decisions are crushing them. The search and rescue mission for purpose has been all but abandoned. They don't know what tomorrow looks like, and they don't know Jesus. But they walk into church and get a little John 3:16. They get a little seed and God begins His incredible work. There's a wife waiting to talk when the husband gets home. Hope gives birth. Pills are thrown out. Magazines are trashed. Kids are communicated with. A small group is joined, and on and on and on God moves. It's how the Kingdom works. It's how Jesus wants His Kingdom to work in your life beyond a Sunday morning. Through gloriously small, unpredictable, and unlikely ways, He'll get the glory, and you'll get out of the bigger and better trap so you can simply follow Jesus.

Will you quit being a Christian to simply follow Jesus? Are you tired yet of the games, politics, and lifeless music emanating from church building after church building? There has got to be more, doesn't there? You know there is. So what are you waiting for? Dr. Luke has given Theophilus and all of us a lot to consider. Revive your certainty of faith. Begin living expectantly. Shape your vision with Jesus's mission. Adjust your quest for the spectacular. Stop trying to be the expert. Begin believing eternal life is for now. Learn how to navigate storms. Stop settling for less. Decide to serve and help. Smell like Jesus. Live in God's presence. Don't drive forward in reverse. Remember, size DOES matter!

THAT should keep you busy for a while! Maybe in the meantime you'll find meaning again in being a Jesus follower. Perhaps you'll even help our fond label of "Christian" make a cultural comeback not seen since New Kids On The Block began advertising Grecian Formula.

The power of Jesus's name has actually never been dialed back. We somehow mistakenly took the label of "Christian" and made it void of Jesus. Your Holy Spirit angst and Jesus living through you will help a hurting world see how Jesus is Lord no matter what brand we wear. That's why I quit being a Christian to follow Jesus. I hope you'll join me.

Chapter End Notes

1. Dallas Willard, The Divine Conspiracy: Rediscovering Our Hidden Life In God, (New York, NY; HarperCollins 1997).

Acknowledgements

For several years there's been some malaise in western church world. Something is just off, and many pastors, counselors, authors, and frustrated "common folk" have been writing furiously. In *Mere Christianity*, C.S. Lewis once wrote, "A Christian society is not going to arrive until most of us really want it: and we are not going to want it until we become fully Christian." THAT is what so many church leaders are trying to figure out.

I tend to read a lot and take it all in. This book is the result of not being able to take it any longer. After taking the Kingdom folks at Cumberland Community Church on a long and probably tedious trek through the book of Luke, I decided to write. The powerful foundations laid by a first century doctor named Luke became my jumping off point to craft a sermon series and eventually this book.

When I prepare a sermon, I read voraciously. I want to read as much and as varied content as I can within a week's time. I go to Timothy Keller a lot. I still think Max Lucado is brilliant. There are bits and pieces I still lift from Rick Warren because he's still on purpose. Before the whole hell heresy thing, I took in my fair share of Rob Bell. Don't judge me.

I like John Ortberg, Bill Hybels, Kyle Idleman, David Platt, Francis Chan, and Matt Chandler. I can also go a bit old school with guys like N.T. Wright, Os Guiness, Dallas Willard, Henri Nouwen, John Stott, C.S. Lewis, R.C. Sproul, and Oswald Chambers.

Each week I pour in about 25 hours to painfully birth my Sunday morning message. Along with several commentaries, I read sermons from guys like John MacArthur, Mark Driscoll, and a host of other brilliant "unknowns" I've found at SermonCentral.com and Monergism.com.

I absolutely love to explore and discover Jewish contextual insights from people like Lois Tverberg, Ray Vanderlaan, and David Bivins --- from places like Egrc.net, Followtherabbi.com, and Jerusalemperspective.com.

All this to simply say, "Sometimes I don't know what's me or what's not." My good friend and author, Curt Coffman, once jokingly told me to quote somebody three times, and then it's mine! I try to give credit to where credit is due, but so much of my thinking, wordsmithing, and inner shaping come from so many brilliant people. I thank them all.

I DO know where definitive credit should be given. It's to my wife and kids who have allowed me to do my thing for nearly 30 years. Crazy. Sherry is one of THE best pastor's wives I know. She's smokin' hot too. Brooklynn, Lauren, Morgan, and Michael all love God, the Church, and are serving well --- mostly with their music. They are amazing PK's like none other. Great kids allow dads like me to do some pretty cool things. Along with Patti Terrell, my daughter Brooklynn helped edit and sharpen this work.

The staff and elders (and their awesome spouses) at Cumberland Community Church gave me time and grace to complete this book. Thanks Rob Irvine, Joe Braun, Jen Overly, Megan Sullivan, Kyle

Nighman, Ben Propst, Mitzi Gresham, Mike Thurman, Chris Case, Jeremy Hazelton, Loary Coates, Angel Crow, Brea Lavin, Doug Scott, Kevin Cash, Kevin Hammond, Jon Franz, Kevin Hambrick, Chuck Dunlop, Victor Boney, Doug Bentle, Terence Allen, Rob Kischuk, Jay Overstreet, Vince Groff, Frank Sullivan, Marty Esterman, Gaius Gough, Josh Keller, Brian McCormick, and James Garrett. The congregation at CCC gave me the grace to practice the contents even when mistakes were glaringly obvious and omitted from these carefully edited pages. Oh... and what about the smokin' front and back cover designs which magically compelled you to try this thing in the first place? Kacy Fabie and Freedom Rodriguez are to thank. I humbly owe a debt of gratitude towards all of the above-mentioned Jesus followers. Thanks ya'll!

Lastly (which Biblically means first), to the One who chose me, adopted me, redeemed me, and calls me His precious possession... I am humbled to be used in any way, much less to write a ding dang book. My salvation, sanctification, transformation, and not being left at the train station is HIS work, not mine. Anything I have to offer can only be pointed to Jesus's amazing grace, which, seems to never run dry despite my best efforts at trashing it.

I am such a screw up. I have stumbled forward over the years. God has surrounded me with great people. Jesus has chosen the foolish to confound the world. This book remains as obvious evidence.

I'd love to hear from you with any feedback. You can catch me on Facebook, or e-mail at: **alanrayscott@yahoo.com**
Thanks for reading. Blessings!

About The Author

Since 2006, Alan Scott has been one of the pastors at Cumberland Community Church in Smyrna, Georgia. God has used Alan and a team of people to turn this once attractional church into an authentic community church attempting to transform Smyrna, Atlanta, and the world. Previous to this assignment, Alan was a teaching pastor in Denver, a pastor in Indiana, church planter in Georgia, and a youth pastor in Ohio.

On May 9, 1987, Alan graduated from Cincinnati Christian University with an English Bible degree. He married his college love, Sherry, on that same day. Alan and Sherry have four kids: Brooklynn, Lauren, Morgan, and Michael.

In 2005, Alan published: "It's A God-Thing... Miracle In A Cornfield."

You can check out Alan's video sermons and blogs at: **www.cumberlandchurch.org**. You can also catch up with Alan on Facebook at: **https://www.facebook.com/alanrayscott** and on Twitter @ alanrayscott.

(From L-R: Morgan, Michael, Brooklynn, Lauren,
Sherry, & Alan Scott – circa 2013)